I0114541

	Report		Information		Corroboration/Analyst Notes
	2016/80 *6/20/16 **9/19/16		"Russian regime has been cultivating, supporting and assisting TRUMP for at least 5 years. Aim, endorsed by PUTIN, has been to encourage splits and divisions in western alliance"		Trump was in St. Petersburg in 1987 working on a real-estate deal, and in 2008 Trump claimed to have been to Russia six times in 18 months. Though he did not mention St. Petersburg, the real estate deal he was negotiating included a hotel in St. Petersburg.[1,2] In 2013, Trump hosted a pageant in Moscow, and according to the Washington Post, Aras Agalarov served as a liaison between Trump and Putin. At the pageant and its after party, Trump claimed, "Almost all of the oligarchs were in the room." In the same article the Washington Post reported that in 2008, Donald Trump, Jr., claimed, "Russians make up a disproportionate cross-section of a lot of our assets."[3]
	2016/80 *6/20/16 **9/19/16		"So far TRUMP has declined various sweetener real estate business deals offered him in Russia in order to further the Kremlin's cultivation of him."		Trump was in St. Petersburg in 1987 working on a real-estate deal, and in 2008 Trump claimed to have been to Russia six times in 18 months. Though he did not mention St. Petersburg, the real estate deal he was negotiating included a hotel in St. Petersburg.[4,5] In 2013, Trump hosted a pageant in Moscow, and according to the Washington Post, Aras Agalarov served as a liaison between Trump and Putin. At the pageant and its after party, Trump claimed, "Almost all of the oligarchs were in the room." In the same article the Washington Post reported that in 2008, Donald Trump, Jr., claimed, "Russians make up a disproportionate cross-section of a lot of our assets."[6]
	2016/80 *6/20/16 **9/19/16		"However, he and his inner circle have accepted a regular flow of intelligence from the Kremlin, including on his Democratic and other political rivals"		
	2016/80 *6/20/16 **9/19/16		"Former top Russian intelligence officer claims FSB has compromised TRUMP through his activities in Moscow sufficiently to be able to blackmail him. According to several knowledgeable sources, his conduct in Moscow has included		This information was provided by ▮Primary Subsource's▮ sub-source. The sub-source has been identified as ▮Primary Subsource's subsource Primary Subsource's source identifying▮

*Report Date
**Date Report Provided to FBI by Steele

Report Provided to Journalists, Not FBI
Report Not Provided to Corn

Declassified by FBI - C58W88B61
on 10/8/2020
This redacted version only

SENATE-FISA2020-001586

	Report		Information		Corroboration/Analyst Notes
			perverted sexual acts which have been arranged/monitored by FSB"		On **Date** 2017, a **Sources and** reported to FBI ▮ that **Individual 1** was attempting to provide information about a **Individual 2** **Identifies Individual 2** The **Individual 2** claimed to have compromising tapes on President Donald Trump.[7] *[Analyst Note: It is unknown if the tapes mentioned in this reporting are the same tapes mentioned in report 80. The only similar information is the use of "tapes"* **Identifies Individual 2** ▮
					Individual 1 who is a **Identifies Individual 1** ▮
					▮ An uncorroborated source, journalist and author Andrea Chalupa, was cited in an Australian magazine article dated 1 November 2016 as mentioning Trump having an orgy in Russia.[9]
					▮ The details in the **Steele** reporting differ somewhat from the Australian reporting ("golden showers" versus "orgies"), although these differences may have been a result of how the writers decided to characterize the information.
	2016/80 *6/20/16 **9/19/16		"A dossier of compromising material on Hillary CLINTON has been collated by the Russian Intelligence Services over many years and mainly comprises bugged conversations she had on various visits to Russia and intercepted phone calls rather than embarrassing conduct. The dossier is controlled by chief Kremlin spokesman, PESKOV..."		▮ This information was provided by **Primary Subsource's** sub-source. The sub-source has been identified as **Primary Subsource's subsource identifies Primary Subsource and subsou** ▮
					▮ Dmitriy Peskov is Deputy Head and Press Secretary, Presidential Administration since 2012.

*Report Date
Date Report Provided to FBI by **Steele

Report Provided to Journalists, Not FBI
Report Not Provided to Corn

	Report		Information		Corroboration/Analyst Notes
			Version sent to FBI: "... on direct orders from Putin. It has not been distributed abroad as yet, including to TRUMP team; but PUTIN's intentions for its use remain unclear." *Version sent to Journalists:* "...directly on Putin's orders. However, it has not as yet been distributed abroad, including to TRUMP. Russian intentions for its deployment still unclear."		Other Agency Reporting ▮▮▮ ▮ As US Secretary of State, Hillary Clinton took four trips to Russia (one each in 2009 and 2010, and two in 2012).[14] Bill Clinton met with Boris Yeltsin 18 times while serving as President, but it is unclear how many times the first lady accompanied him on those trips.[15]
	2016/80 *6/20/16 **9/19/16		▮ "1. Speaking to a trusted compatriot in June 2016 sources A and B, a senior Russian Foreign Ministry figure and a former top-level Russian intelligence officer still active inside the Kremlin respectively, the Russian authorities had been cultivating and supporting US Republican presidential candidate, DONALD TRUMP for at least 5 years. Source B asserted that the TRUMP operation was both supported and directed by Russian President Vladimir PUTIN. Its aim was to sow discord and disunity both within the US itself, but more especially within the Transatlantic alliance which was viewed as inimical to Russia's interests. Source C, a senior Russian financial official said the TRUMP operation should be seen in terms of PUTIN's desire to return to Nineteenth Century 'Great Power' politics, anchored upon countries' interests rather than the ideals-based international order established after World War Two. S/he had overheard PUTIN talking in this way to close associates on several occasions."		▮ This information was provided by ▮▮▮Primary Subsource's▮▮▮ sub-source. The sub-source has been identified as ▮▮▮Primary Subsource's subsource identifies Primary Subsource and subsource▮▮▮ ▮▮ ▮ No direct mention of the "Great Game" could be found in Putin's public speeches, including his annual address to the Valdai Discussion Club. However, there is plenty of media attention and analysis paid to his "19th century outlook." This outlook can be viewed in the context of his speeches "Presidential Address to the Federal Assembly"[16] "Message from the President of Russia to the leaders of several European countries"[17] and "Vladimir Putin's Interview with Radio Europe 1 and TF1 TV Channel."[18]

*Report Date
**Date Report Provided to FBI by ▮Steele▮

Report Provided to Journalists, Not FBI
Report Not Provided to Corn

PRODUCED TO SJC/SSCI

	Report		Information		Corroboration/Analyst Notes
					Trump was in St. Petersburg in 1987 working on a real-estate deal, and in 2008 Trump claimed to have been to Russia six times in 18 months. Though he did not mention St. Petersburg, the real estate deal he was negotiating included a hotel in St. Petersburg.[19, 20] In 2013, Trump hosted a pageant in Moscow, and according to the Washington Post, Aras Agalarov served as a liaison between Trump and Putin. At the pageant and its after party, Trump claimed, "Almost all of the oligarchs were in the room." In the same article the Washington Post reported that in 2008, Donald Trump, Jr., claimed, "Russians make up a disproportionate cross-section of a lot of our assets."[21]
	2016/80 *6/20/16 **9/19/16		"2. In terms of specifics, Source A confided that the Kremlin had been feeding TRUMP and his team valuable intelligence on his opponents…" ***Version sent to FBI:*** "…, including Democratic presidential candidate Hillary Clinton,…" ***Version sent to Journalists:*** [omitted] "…for several years (see more below). This was confirmed by Source D, a close associate of TRUMP who had organized and managed his recent trips to Moscow, and who reported, also in June 2016, that this Russian intelligence had been "very helpful." The Kremlin's cultivation operation on TRUMP also had comprised offering him various lucrative real estate development business deals in Russia, especially in relation to the ongoing 2018 World Cup soccer tournament. However, so far, for reasons unknown, TRUMP had not taken up any of these."		Trump was in St. Petersburg in 1987 working on a real-estate deal, and in 2008 Trump claimed to have been to Russia six times in 18 months. Though he did not mention St. Petersburg, the real estate deal he was negotiating included a hotel in St. Petersburg.[22, 23] In 2013, Trump hosted a pageant in Moscow, and according to the Washington Post, Aras Agalarov served as a liaison between Trump and Putin. At the pageant and its after party, Trump claimed, "Almost all of the oligarchs were in the room." In the same article the Washington Post reported that in 2008, Donald Trump, Jr., claimed, "Russians make up a disproportionate cross-section of a lot of our assets."[24] Other Agency Reporting ▮▮▮ [25]
	2016/80 *6/20/16 **9/19/16		"3. However, there were other aspects to TRUMP's engagement with the Russian authorities. One which had borne fruit for them was to exploit TRUMP's personal obsessions and sexual perversion in order to obtain suitable 'kompromat' (compromising material) on him. According to Source D, where s/he had been present, TRUMP's (perverted) conduct in Moscow included hiring the presidential suite of the Ritz Carlton Hotel, where he knew President and Mrs OBAMA		This information was provided by ▮▮▮ Primary Subsource's ▮ sub-source. The sub-source has been identified as ▮ Primary Subsource's subsource identifies Primary Subsource and ▮ ▮▮▮ There is no confirmation that Trump stayed here. There is no "Presidential Suite" currently listed on the Ritz Carlton website, though they do have the Moscow Suite, Ritz-Carlton Suite, Carlton

*Report Date
**Date Report Provided to FBI by Steele

Report Provided to Journalists, Not FBI
Report Not Provided to Corn

	Report		Information		Corroboration/Analyst Notes
			(whom he hated) had stayed on one of their official trips to Russia, and defiling the bed where they had slept by employing a number of prostitutes to perform a 'golden showers' (urination) show in front of him. The hotel was known to be under FSB control with microphones and concealed cameras in all the main rooms to record anything they wanted to."		Suite, Teverskaya Suite, and the Executive Suite.[26] There is mention of a Presidential Suite at the Ritz Carlton in a press release from 2015.[27] ■ In 2009 President Obama stayed in the Presidential suite at the Ritz-Carlton Hotel in Moscow which is described as a five room kremlin view luxury suite with huge panoramic windows.[28] ▮Other Agency Reporting▮
■	2016/80 *6/20/16 **9/19/16	■	"4. The Moscow Ritz Carlton episode involving TRUMP reported above was confirmed by Source E, a senior (western) member of staff at the hotel, who said that s/he and several of the staff were aware of it at the time and subsequently. S/he believed it had happened in 2013. Source E provided an introduction for a company ethnic Russian operative to Source F, a female staffer at the hotel when TRUMP had stayed there, who also confirmed the story. Speaking separately in June 2016, Source B (the former top-level Russian intelligence officer) asserted that TRUMP's unorthodox behavior in Russia over the years had provided the authorities there with enough embarrassing material on the now Republican presidential candidate to be able to blackmail him if they so wished."		This information was provided by ▮Primary Subsource's▮ sub-source. The sub-source has been identified as ▮Primary Subsource's subsource identifies Primary Subsource and subsource▮
■	2016/80 *6/20/16 **9/19/16	■	"5. Asked about the Kremlin's reported intelligence feed to TRUMP over recent years and rumours about a Russian dossier of 'kompromat' on Hillary CLINTON (being circulated), Source B confirmed the file's existence. S/he confided in a trusted companion that it had been collated by Department K of the FSB for many years, dating back to her husband Bill's presidency, and comprised mainly eavesdropped conversations of various sorts rather than details/evidence of unorthodox or embarrassing behavior. Some of the conversations were from bugged comments CLINTON had made on her various trips to Russia and focused on things she said which contradicted her		■ This information was provided by ▮Primary Subsource's▮ sub-source. The sub-source has been identified as ▮Primary Subsource's subsource identifies Primary Subsource and subsource▮ ▮Other Agency Reporting▮ 30

*Report Date
**Date Report Provided to FBI by ▮Steele▮

Report Provided to Journalists, Not FBI
Report Not Provided to Corn

█ Report	█ Information	█ Corroboration/Analyst Notes
	current position on various issues. Others were most probably from phone intercepts."	█ This could also be Directorate K of the FSB, "Counterintelligence in Financial Services," which monitors employees in the financial sector.[31] █ As US Secretary of State, Hillary Clinton took four trips to Russia (one each in 2009 and 2010, and two in 2012).[32] Bill Clinton met with Boris Yeltsin 18 times while serving as President, but it is unclear how many times the first lady accompanied him on those trips.[33]
█ 2016/80 *6/20/16 **9/19/16	█ "6. Continuing on this theme, Source G, a senior Kremlin official, confided that…" ***Version sent to FBI:*** "…the CLINTON dossier was controlled exclusively by senior Kremlin spokesman, Dmitriy PESKOV, on the direct instructions of PUTIN himself. The dossier had not been made available, as yet, inter alia, to any foreigners, including TRUMP and his inner circle. However PUTIN's intentions with regard to the dossier and its future dissemination remained unclear." ***Version sent to Journalists:*** "…[t]he CLINTON dossier was controlled exclusively by chief Kremlin spokesman, Dmitriy PESKOV, who was responsible for compiling/handling it on the explicit instructions of PUTIN himself. The dossier however had not as yet been made available abroad, including to TRUMP or his campaign team. At present it was unclear what PUTIN's intentions were in this regard."	█ This information was provided by Primary Subsource's sub-source. The sub-source has been identified as Primary Subsource's subsource identifies Primary Subsource and subs█ **Other Agency Reporting** █ .35, 36, 37 **Other Agency Reporting** █ 38
█ 2016/086 *7/26/15	█ Russia has extensive programme of state-sponsored offensive cyber operations. External targets include foreign	

*Report Date
**Date Report Provided to FBI by Steele

Report Provided to Journalists, Not FBI
Report Not Provided to Corn

PRODUCED TO SJC/SSCI
PRODUCED TO

Report	Information	Corroboration/Analyst Notes
	governments and big corporations, especially banks. FSB leads on cyber within Russian apparatus. Limited success in attacking top foreign targets like G7 governments, security services and IFIs but much more on second tier ones through IT back doors, using corporate and other visitors to Russia.	
2016/086 *7/26/15	FSB often uses coercion and blackmail to recruit most capable cyber operatives in Russia into its state-sponsored programmes. Heavy use also, both wittingly and unwittingly, of CIS emigres working in western corporations and ethnic Russians employed by neighbouring governments e.g. Latvia	
2016/086 *7/26/15	Example cited of successful Russian cyber operation targeting senior Western business visitor. Provided back door into important Western institutions.	
2016/086 *7/26/15	Example given of US citizen of Russian origin approached by FSB and offered incentive of "investment" in his business when visiting Moscow.	
2016/086 *7/26/15	Problems however for Russian authorities themselves in countering local hackers and cyber criminals, operating outside state control. Central Bank claims there were over 20 serious attacks on correspondent accounts held by CBR in 2015, comprising Roubles several billion in fraud.	
2016/086 *7/26/15	Some details given of leading non-state Russian cyber criminal groups	
2016/086 *7/26/15	1. Speaking in June 2016, a number of Russian figures with a detailed knowledge of national cyber crimes, both state-sponsored and otherwise, outlines the current situation in this area. A former senior intelligence officer divided Russian state-sponsored offensive cyber operations into four categories (in order of priority):- targeting foreign, especially western governments; penetrating leading foreign business corporations, especially banks; domestic monitoring of the elite; and attacking political opponents both at home and	

*Report Date
**Date Report Provided to FBI by Steele

Report Provided to Journalists, Not FBI
Report Not Provided to Corn

Report	Information	Corroboration/Analyst Notes
	abroad. The former intelligence officer reported that the Federal Security Service (FSB) was the lead organization within the Russian state apparatus for cyber operations.	
███ 2016/086 *7/26/15	█ 2. In terms of the success of Russian offensive cyber operations to date, a senior government figure reported that there had been only limited success in penetrating the "first tier" foreign targets. These comprised western (especially G7 and NATO) governments, security and intelligence services and central banks, and the IFIs. To compensate for this shortfall, massive effort had been invested, with much greater success, in attacking the "secondary targets", particularly western private banks and the governments of smaller states allied to the West. S/he mentioned Latvia in this regard. Hundreds of agents, either consciously cooperating with the FSB or whose personal and professional IT systems had been unwittingly compromised, were recruited. Many were people who had ethnic and family ties to Russia and/or had been incentivized financially to cooperate. Such people often would receive monetary inducements or contractual favours from the Russian state or its agents in return. This had created difficulties for parts of the Russian state apparatus in obliging/indulging them e.g. the Central Bank of Russia knowingly having to cover up for such agents' money laundering operations through the Russian financial system.	███ This information was provided by ███Primary Subsource's███ sub-source. The sub-source has been identified as ███Primary Subsource's subsource identifies Primary Subsource and s████████████████████████
███ 2016/086 *7/26/15	█ 3. In terms of the FSB's recruitment of capable cyber operatives to carry out its, ideally deniable, offensive cyber operations, a Russian IT specialist with direct knowledge reported in June 2016 that this was often done using coercion and blackmail. In terms of 'foreign' agents, the FSB was approaching US citizens of Russian (Jewish) origin on business trips to Russia. In one case a US citizen of Russian ethnicity had been visiting Moscow to attract investors in his new	███ This information was provided by ███Primary Subsource's███ sub-source. The sub-source has been identified as ███Primary Subsource's subsource identifies Primary Subsource and s███████████████████

*Report Date
**Date Report Provided to FBI by ███Steele███

Report Provided to Journalists, Not FBI
Report Not Provided to Corn

■ Report	■ Information	■ Corroboration/Analyst Notes
	information technology program. The FSB clearly knew this and had offered to provide seed capital to this person in return for them being able to access and modify his IP, with a view to targeting priority foreign targets by planting a Trojan virus in the software. The US visitor was told this was common practice. The FSB also had implied significant operational success as a result of installing cheap Russian IT games containing their own malware unwittingly by targets on their PCs and other platforms.	
	■ 4. In a more advanced and successful FSB operation, an IT operator inside a leading Russian SOE, who previously had been employed on conventional (defensive) IT work there, had been under instruction for the last year to conduct an offensive cyber operation against a foreign director of the company. Although the latter was apparently an infrequent visitor to Russia, the FSB now successfully had penetrated his personal IT and through this had managed to access various important institutions in the West through the back door.	
■ 2016/086 *7/26/15	■ 5. In terms of other technical IT platforms, as FSB cyber operative flagged up the 'Telegram' enciphered commercial system as having been of especial concern and therefore heavily targeted by the FSB, not least because it was used frequently by Russian internal political activities and oppositionists. His/her understanding was that the FSB now successfully had cracked this communications software and therefore it was no longer secure to use.	■ This information was provided by Primary Subsource's sub-source. The sub-source was identified was Primary Subsource's subsource identifies Primary Subource and subsource
■ 2016/086 *7/26/15	■ 6. The senior Russian government figure cited above also reported that non-state sponsored cyber crime was becoming an increasing problem inside Russia for the government and authorities there. The Central Bank of Russia claimed that in 2015 alone there had been more than 20 attempts at serious cyber embezzlement of money from corresponding accounts held there, comprising several billions Roubles. More generally, s/he understood there were circa 15 major organized crime	

*Report Date
**Date Report Provided to FBI by Steele

Report Provided to Journalists, Not FBI
Report Not Provided to Corn

▮ Report	▮ Information	▮ Corroboration/Analyst Notes
	groups in the country involved cyber crime, all of which continued to operate largely outside state and FSB control. These include the so-called 'Anunak', 'Buktrap' and 'Metel' organisations.	
▮ 2016/94 *7/19/16 **9/19/16	▮ "Speaking in July 2016...Igor SECHIN confided the details of a recent secret meeting between him and visiting Foreign Affairs Advisor...Carter Page"	▮ This information was provided by ▮Primary Subsource's sub-source. The sub-source was identified as ▮Primary Subsource's subsource identifies Primary Subsource and subsource▮

Sources and Methods [39]

- Sequestered by court order

- Sequestered by court order [40,41]

[42,43]

- ▮ *PAGE worked as Gazprom as a "Corporate Broker" which is Corporate Investment Marketing. During that time, he was instrumental in instituting an investor's day. PAGE attended the Gazprom Investor's day on 02/28/2017 in Singapore. When asked by FBI NY who from Gazprom he met at the event, PAGE said he thought the CFO was there*[44].

- Sequestered by court order

[45,46,47]

- Sequestered by court order

*Report Date
**Date Report Provided to FBI by ▮Steele

Report Provided to Journalists, Not FBI
Report Not Provided to Corn

■ Report	■ Information	■ Corroboration/Analyst Notes
		Sequestered by court order

Sequestered by court order [48]

- Sequestered by court order [49]

- Sequestered by court order [50]

- [51] Valery L. Marakov PII _____ is the President and Professor of Economics at NES. He is part of the faculty there and has been a lifelong academic. [52]

■ "Though he publicly attended the [July 2016 New Economic School] event, Page refused to answer questions about his itinerary in Moscow. The media criticized him for specifically avoiding questions about his plans to meet with GOR officials." [53]

■ Page reported to have met with Deputy Prime Minister Arkady Dvorkovich at NES. [54]

■ In December of 2016, Page visited the NES again. He had dinner with Schlomo and Yuval Weber, and Andrej Krickovic. During the dinner, DPM Dvorkovich congratulated Page on Trump's victory, and asked about how to connect for future cooperation. Page told Dvorkovich that he was no longer involved with the Campaign. [55]

■ On 16 March 2017, Page told FBI NY that he was invited to speak at the NES by Weber. Page received permission from Corey Lewandowski to attend the NES graduation and give the commencement speech. Page offered to have Trump do the speech instead; the campaign refused. Page, according to the e-mail, was to attend outside of his

*Report Date
**Date Report Provided to FBI by Steele

Report Provided to Journalists, Not FBI
Report Not Provided to Corn

SENATE-FISA2020-001596

▮ Report	▮ Information	▮ Corroboration/Analyst Notes
		campaign role. Page stated JD Gordon "never said no, but expressed it wasn't a good idea," to participate. [56] ▮▮▮ **Other Agency Reporting** ▮▮▮ [57]
▮ 2016/94 *7/19/16 **9/19/16	▮ "In July 2016...DIVYEKIN also had met secretly with PAGE on his recent visit..."	▮ This information was provided by Primary Subsource's sub-source. The sub-source has been identified as Primary Subsource's subsource identifies Primary Subsource and subso ▮▮▮ **Other Agency Reporting** ▮▮▮ **Other Agency Reporting** ▮▮▮ " [60]

*Report Date
**Date Report Provided to FBI by Steele

Report Provided to Journalists, Not FBI
Report Not Provided to Corn

PRODUCED TO SJC/SSCI

Report	Information	Corroboration/Analyst Notes
		On 23 March 2015, an article in Gazeta.ru detailed the departure of Oleg Morozov, the head of the Russian Presidential Administration's Domestic Policy Administration. Morozov, who had served in the position since May 2012, was replaced by Tatyana Voronova. In turn, the article named Igor Diveykin, "current leader of [first deputy head of the Presidential Staff Vyacheslav] Volodin's secretariat."[61]
		On 23 September 2016, Yahoo News published an article claiming Carter Page was under investigation by the FBI and US Intelligence due to his ties with Russia. This article mentioned Page's alleged meeting with Divyekin.[62]
		Sequestered by court order
		Sequestered by court order [66]
2016/94 *7/19/16 **9/19/16	"[SECHIN] had raised with PAGE the issues of future bilateral energy cooperation and prospects for an associated move to lift Ukraine-related western sanctions against Russia."	This information was provided by Primary Subsource's sub-source. The sub-source was identified as Primary Subsource's subsource identifies Primary Subsource and subsource
		In a September 2014 interview, Igor Sechin was quoted saying "Neither I nor my company have anything to do with the crisis in Ukraine. As such, there is no foundation for the sanctions against me and Rosneft. They represent a violation of international law."[67]
2016/95 *Jul/Aug 16 **9/19/16	"Close associate of Donald TRUMP, admitted that there was a well-developed conspiracy of co-operation between them and the Russian leadership. This was managed on the TRUMP	On 16 March 2017, Page told FBI NY Ed Cox introduced Page to Corey Lewandowski in January of 2016. Lewandowski then introduced Page to the Deputy Campaign Manager Michael Glassner. Glassner

*Report Date
**Date Report Provided to FBI by Steele

Report Provided to Journalists, Not FBI
Report Not Provided to Corn

On 16 March 2017, Page told FBI NY that he never met nor spoke to Paul Manafort.

▮ Report	▮ Information	▮ Corroboration/Analyst Notes
	side by the Republican candidate's campaign manager, Paul MANAFORT, who was using foreign policy advisor, Carter PAGE, and others as intermediaries."	introduced Page to Sam Clovis. The first public announcement of Page's participation in the Campaign came in March of 2016. [68] ▮ On 16 March 2017, Page told FBI NY that he never met nor spoke to Paul Manafort. There was one email in which Manafort was a party to a reply-all email by Page. Page signed Non-Disclosure Agreements with the Trump Campaign and Global Partners in Democracy. PAGE did not attend any Principles' meetings. [69] Sequestered by court order [70] Sequestered by court order [71] ▮ On 16 March 2017 Page told FBI NY after the attention that Page received from his NES speech, Burt Mizusawa and Joe Schmitz both asked Page to keep a low profile. PAGE was also told by Boris Epstheyn that he was still in the "orbit" of the campaign. [72]
▮ 2016/95 *Jul/Aug 16 **9/19/16	▮ "Source E acknowledged that the Russian regime had been behind the recent leak of embarrassing e-mail messages emanating from the Democratic National Committee (DNC), to the WikiLeaks platform."	▮ ▮ In October 2016, the United States Government officially blamed Russia for interfering with the election process and assisting with the DNC hacks that occurred earlier in the year. Open Source

*Report Date
**Date Report Provided to FBI by Steele

Report Provided to Journalists, Not FBI
Report Not Provided to Corn

PRODUCED TO SJC/SSCI

	Report		Information		Corroboration/Analyst Notes
					reporting about Russia's potential involvement in the DNC hack began to appear in media outlets since late July 2016. [73,74,75]

On 10 March 2017, Roger Stone spoke with *The Washington Times* and acknowledged he had been in contact with Guccifer 2.0, an entity tied to the DNC hack, via Twitter direct message (DM). Stone provided a copy of the DM to *The Washington Times*. [76]

The Washington Times provided the following overview of the DM exchange between Stone and Guccifer:

- On 14 August 2016, Stone DM'd Guccifer and stated he was *"delighted"* to see the user's twitter handle reinstated after having been suspended.
- On 16 August 2016, Stone sent a DM asking Guccifer to retweet an article he had written regarding the *'rigg[ing]'* of the 2016 presidential elections.

- Guccifer later replied to Stone stating: *"wow. thank u for writing back, and thank u for an article about me!!! did you find anything interesting in the docs I posted"*
- On 17 August 2016, Guccifer sent a DM to Stone stating *"i'm pleased to say u r great man. please tell me if I can help u anyhow. It would be a great pleasure to me."*

	Report	Information	Corroboration/Analyst Notes
	2016/95 *Jul/Aug 16 **9/19/16	"In return the TRUMP team had agreed to sideline Russian intervention in Ukraine as a campaign issue and to raise US/NATO defence commitment in the Baltics and Eastern Europe to deflect attention away from Ukraine"	Sensitive FBI Information [77]

*Report Date
**Date Report Provided to FBI by Steele

Report Provided to Journalists, Not FBI
Report Not Provided to Corn

PRODUCED TO SJC/SSCI

▮ Report	▮ Information	▮ Corroboration/Analyst Notes
		Sequestered by court order
		▮ On 16 March 2017, Page provided FBI NY the 07/14/2016 e-mail received from JD Gordon informing of the policy change. Page said that he had no part in the decision, but he supported it. Page assessed that JD Gordon was controlling and Gordon did not disclose much of his decisions to the team. PAGE later stated that he felt that Manafort more-likely-than-not recommended the pro-Russian changes.[79]
		▮ In July 2016, during the RNC in Cleveland, members of the Trump campaign convinced the platform committee to change [Diana] Denman's proposal. It went from calling on the U.S to provide Ukraine "lethal defensive weapons" to the phrase "appropriate assistance."[80]
		▮ "'They were over sitting in chairs at the side of the room,' Denman said of two men who said they were working for the Trump campaign, one of whom was [J.D] Gordon. 'When I read my amendment, they got up and walked over and talked to the co-chairman and they read it. That's when I was told that it was going to be tabled.'"[81]
		▮ On 21 July 2016, Trump discussed NATO by saying, "If we cannot be properly reimbursed for the tremendous cost of our military protecting other countries, and in many cases the countries I'm talking about are extremely rich. Then if we cannot make a deal, which I believe we will be able to, and which I would prefer being able to, but if we cannot make a deal, I would like you to say, I would prefer being able to, some people, the one thing they took out of your last story, you know, some

*Report Date
**Date Report Provided to FBI by Steele

Report Provided to Journalists, Not FBI
Report Not Provided to Corn

▮ Report	▮ Information	▮ Corroboration/Analyst Notes
		people, the fools and the haters, they said "Oh, Trump doesn't want to protect you." I would prefer that we be able to continue, but if we are not going to be reasonably reimbursed for the tremendous cost of protecting these massive nations with tremendous wealth."[82]
▮ 2016/95 *Jul/Aug 16 **9/19/16	▮ "Intelligence network being used against CLINTON comprised three elements. Firstly there were agents/facilitators within the Democratic Party structure itself; secondly Russian émigré and associated offensive cyber operators based in the U.S; and thirdly, state-sponsored cyber operatives working in Russia."	▮▮ State-sponsored cyber operatives and the evidence suggesting Russia had knowledge and operational input.[83] ▮ Open source reporting indicates that the hacking done by Guccifer 2.0 was done in consistency to the Russian interests and activities concerning the United States.[84]
▮ 2016/95 *Jul/Aug 16 **9/19/16	▮ "Unlike in Russia, [CHINA] these were substantial and involved the payment of large bribes and kickbacks which, were they to become public, would be potentially very damaging to their campaign"	▮ While there is no reporting of bribery and kickbacks to China, the references below demonstrate how the Trump campaign discussed and interacted with China during the campaign: ▮ "On June 28 during a speech in Pennsylvania, U.S., GOP presidential candidate Donald Trump brought forward his plan to bring jobs back to the United States. He attacked Hillary Clinton and criticized China, vowing to start an unrelenting offensive against Chinese economic practices."[85] ▮ As of 24 October 2016, according to a Telegraph investigation, "Donald Trump's presidential campaign is facing a fundraising scandal after a Telegraph investigation exposed how key supporters were prepared to accept illicit donations from foreign backers. Senior figures involved with the Great America PAC, one of the leading "independent" groups organizing television advertisements and grassroots support for the Republican nominee, sought to channel $2 million from a Chinese donor into the campaign to elect the billionaire despite laws prohibiting donations from foreigners."[86] ▮ As of 14 November 2016, Xi Jinping calls to congratulate Donald Trump. Trump is quoted as saying "China is a great and important country, and China's development is remarkable...The US and China can

*Report Date
**Date Report Provided to FBI by Steele

Report Provided to Journalists, Not FBI
Report Not Provided to Corn

	Report		Information		Corroboration/Analyst Notes
					achieve mutual benefits and win-win results. I would love to work with you to enhance the cooperation between US and China"[87]
					As of November 2016, on the Donald Trump Official website, there is an outline of a 7 Point Plan on American Economy: "5. Instruct the Treasury Secretary to label China a currency manipulator. 6. Instruct the U.S Trade Representative to bring trade cases against China, both in this country and at the WTO...7. Use every lawful presidential power to remedy trade disputes if China does not stop its illegal activities, including theft of American Trade secrets...[38]
	2016/97 *7/30/16		"Kremlin concerned that political fallout from DNC email hacking operation is spiraling out of control"		There were several open source articles published in the months leading up to 30 July 2016. Key open source articles linking Russia and the Trump team were published on the 30 March 2016, 4 April 2016, 18 April 2016, 26 April 2016, 20 July 2016, 21 July 2016, and 25 July 2016.[89]
	2016/97 *7/30/16		"Extreme nervousness among Trump's associates as result of negative media attention/accusations"		Sequestered by court order There were several open source articles published in the months leading up to 30 July 2016. Key open source articles linking Russia and the Trump team were published on the 30 March 2016, 4 April 2016, 18 April 2016, 26 April 2016, 20 July 2016, 21 July 2016, and 25 July 2016.[90]
	2016/97 *7/30/16		"Russians meanwhile keen to cool situation and maintain 'plausible deniability' of existing/ongoing pro-Trump and anti-Clinton operations. Therefore unlikely to be any ratcheting up offensive plays in immediate future"		
	2016/97 *7/30/16		"Source [REDACTED] confirms regular exchange with Kremlin has existed for at least 8 years, including intelligence fed to Russia on oligarchs' activities in US"		On 10 November 2016, Russian Deputy Foreign minister Sergei Rybokev stated that Russia has been in contact with Trump's campaign and will continue these contacts into the administration.[31] There is open source reporting indicating that Trump traveled to Russia in 1987 and that his son Donald Jr. traveled to Moscow in 2008.

*Report Date

**Date Report Provided to FBI by Steele

Report Provided to Journalists, Not FBI

Report Not Provided to Corn

SENATE-FISA2020-001603

	Report		Information		Corroboration/Analyst Notes
					Trump also attended the Miss Universe Pageant in Moscow in 2013.[92] In 2013, Trump hosted a pageant in Moscow, and according to the Washington Post, Aras Agalarov served as a liaison between Trump and Putin. At the pageant and its after party, Trump claimed, "Almost all of the oligarchs were in the room." In the same article the Washington Post reported that in 2008, Donald Trump, Jr., claimed, "Russians make up a disproportionate cross-section of a lot of our assets."[93] ▮ Trump's connections to oligarchs may include Dmitriy Rybolovlev, who purchased mansion from Trump in Miami in July 2014 through a broker named Daniel Tzinker ▮PII▮ who may be connected to several Russian oligarchs.[94] ▮ Dmitriy Rybolovlev is a Russian billionaire who lives in Monaco. He owns real-estate and a portion of the AS Monaco Football Club.[95]
	2016/97 *7/30/16		"1. [REDACTED] high level of anxiety within the Trump team as a result of various accusations leveled against them and indications from the Kremlin that President Putin and others in the leadership thought things had gone too far now and risked spiraling out of control."		▮ Sequestered by court order ▮ ▮ No relevant reporting found RE "gone too far" information as of 14 November 2016.
	2016/97 *7/30/16		"2. [REDACTED] Kremlin wanted the situation to calm but for 'plausible deniability' to be maintained concerning its (extensive) pro-Trump and anti-Clinton operations [REDACTED]"		
	2016/97 *7/30/16		"3. [REDACTED] confirmed that an intelligence exchange had been running between them for at least 8 years. Within this context Putin's priority requirement had been for intelligence on the activities, business and otherwise, in the US of leading Russian oligarchs and their families. Trump and his associates duly had obtained and supplied the Kremlin with this information."		▮ This information was provided by ▮Primary Subsource's subsour▮ to ▮Primary Subsource▮ [ANALYST NOTE: ▮Primary Subsource▮ only had a single, 10-15 minute phone call with an individual who didn't identify himself but who, given the context, ▮Primary Subsource▮ still believes to have been ▮Primary Subsource's subsource▮

*Report Date
**Date Report Provided to FBI by ▮Steele▮

Report Provided to Journalists, Not FBI
Report Not Provided to Corn

▮ Report	▮ Information	▮ Corroboration/Analyst Notes
		▮ On 10 November 2016, Russian Deputy Foreign minister Sergei Rybokev stated that Russia has been in contact with Trump's campaign and will continue these contacts into the administration.[96] ▮ Trump's connections to oligarchs may include: Dmitriy Rybolovlev, who purchased mansion from Trump in Miami in July 2014 through a broker named Daniel Tzinker PII ▮), who may be connected to several Russian oligarchs.[97] ▮ In 2013, Trump hosted a pageant in Moscow, and according to the Washington Post, Aras Agalarov served as a liaison between Trump and Putin. At the pageant and its after party, Trump claimed, "Almost all of the oligarchs were in the room." In the same article the Washington Post reported that in 2008, Donald Trump, Jr., claimed, "Russians make up a disproportionate cross-section of a lot of our assets."[98]
▮ 2016/97 *7/30/16	▮ "4. [REDACTED] As far as 'kompromat' (compromising information) on Trump were concerned, although there was plenty of this, he understood the Kremlin had given its word that it would not be deployed against the Republican presidential candidate given how helpful and cooperative his team had been over several years, and particularly of late."	
▮ 2016/100 *8/5/16 **9/19/16	▮ "Head of PA Ivanov laments Russian intervention in US presidential election and black PR against Clinton and the DNC. Vows not to supply intelligence to Kremlin PR operatives again. Advocates now sitting tight and denying everything"	▮ This information was provided by a secondary sub-source. The secondary sub-source has been identified as Subsource. Identifies subsource ▮ ▮ In August 2016, Kremlin chief of staff or Chief of Staff of the Presidential Administration Sergey Ivanov,[99] an ally and fellow former KGB officer who had held several key posts in Putin's Russia, was replaced with Anton Vaino, a little-known deputy presidential administration chief in charge of protocol.[100]
▮ 2016/100 *8/5/16 **9/19/16	▮ "Presidential spokesman Peskov the main protagonist in Kremlin campaign to aid Trump and damage Clinton. He is now scared and fears being made scapegoat by leadership for	▮ This information was provided by a secondary sub-source. The secondary sub-source has been identified as Subsource. Identifies subsource ▮

*Report Date
**Date Report Provided to FBI by Steele

Report Provided to Journalists, Not FBI
Report Not Provided to Corn

PRODUCED TO SSCI/CSSCI

Report	Information	Corroboration/Analyst Notes
	backlash in US. Problem compounded by his botched intervention in recent Turkish crisis"	■ Dimitri Peskov has been the Press Secretary for Vladimir Putin since 2012. He speaks fluent Turkish, and often is quoted in Turkish press as the Russian spokesmen. During the Turkish crisis, Peskov did several interviews in July 2016 but always on behalf of the Russian government.[101] ■ On 10 August 2016, Putin and Recep Tayyip Ergodan met to discuss restoring relationship between Russia and Turkey.[102]
■ 2016/100 *8/5/16 **9/19/16	■ "Premier Medvedev's office furious over DNC hacking and associated anti-Russian publicity. Want good relations with US and ability to travel there. Refusing to support or help cover up after Peskov"	■ This information was provided by Primary Subsource's sub-source. The sub-source has been identified as Primary Subsource's subsource identifies Primary Subsource and subsc ▮ ■ There has been media speculation that Medvedev and Putin have a strained relationship, but this might have started before this alleged operation.[103]
■ 2016/100 *8/5/16 **9/19/16	■ "Talk now in Kremlin of Trump withdrawing from presidential race altogether, but this still largely wishful thinking by more liberal elements in Moscow"	
■ 2016/100 *8/5/16 **9/19/16	■ "1. Speaking in early August 2016, two well-placed and established Kremlin sources outlined the divisions and backlash in Moscow arising from the leaking of Democratic National Committee (DNC) emails and the wider pro-Trump operation being conducted in the US. Head of Presidential Administration, Sergei Ivanov, was angry at the recent turn of events. He believed the Kremlin 'team' involved, led by presidential spokesman Dmitriy Peskov, had gone too far in interfering in foreign affairs with their 'elephant in a china shop black PR.' Ivanov claimed always to have opposed the handling and exploitation of intelligence by this PR "team." Following the backlash against such foreign interference in US politics, Ivanov	■ This information was provided by Primary Subsource's sub-source. The sub-source has been identified as Primary Subsource's subsource identifies Primary Subsource and subsc ▮ ■ On 28 July 2016, Peskov reported the following to RIA Novosti: "We do not deal with hackers. We have nothing to do with this activity. As for any direct or indirect accusations against the Kremlin or Russia in general alleging that they can somehow be involved in some cyber-attacks, this is totally absurd and is a vivid example of the use of Russophobia and whipping up Russophobia for election campaign purposes in the USA. This is so absurd that it borders on total idiocy."[104]

*Report Date
**Date Report Provided to FBI by Steele

Report Provided to Journalists, Not FBI
Report Not Provided to Corn

PRODUCED TO SSCI

▮ Report	▮ Information	▮ Corroboration/Analyst Notes
	was advocating that the only sensible course of action now for Russian leadership was to 'sit tight and deny everything.'"	▮ In August 2016, Kremlin chief of staff Sergei Ivanov, an ally and fellow former KGB officer who had held several key posts in Putin's Russia, was replaced with Anton Vaino, a little-known deputy presidential administration chief in charge of protocol.[105] ▮ On 1 August 2016, Ivanov, who was referenced as the head of the SVR press bureau, stated, "We will not comment on such statements by a US presidential candidate." This statement was made to Interfax in response to Clinton's allegations that the Russians were involved with the computer intrusion of the DNC.[106]
▮ 2016/100 *8/5/16 **9/19/16	▮ "2. Continuing on this theme the source close to Ivanov reported that Peskov now was "scared shitless" that he would be scapegoated by Putin and the Kremlin and held responsible for the backlash against Russian political interference in the US election. Ivanov was determined to stop Peskov playing an independent role in relation to the US going forward and the source fully expected the presidential spokesman now to lay low. Peskov's position was not helped by a botched attempt by him also to interfere in the recent failed coup in Turkey from a government relations (GR) perspective (no further details)."	▮ This information was provided by ▮Primary Subsource's sub-source. The sub-source has been identified as ▮▮▮ ▮ On 28 July 2016, Peskov reported the following to RIA Novosti: "We do not deal with hackers. We have nothing to do with this activity. As for any direct or indirect accusations against the Kremlin or Russia in general alleging that they can somehow be involved in some cyber-attacks, this is totally absurd and is a vivid example of the use of Russophobia and whipping up Russophobia for election campaign purposes in the USA. This is so absurd that it borders on total idiocy."[107] ▮ Dimitri Peskov has been the Press Secretary for Vladimir Putin since 2012. He speaks fluent Turkish, and often is quoted in Turkish press as the Russian spokesmen. During the Turkish crisis, Peskov did several interviews in July 2016 but always on behalf of the Russian government.[108]
▮ 2016/100 *8/5/16 **9/19/16	▮ "3. The extent of disquiet and division within Moscow caused by the backlash against Russian interference in the US election was underlined by a second source, close to premier Dmitriy Medvedev (DAM). S/he said the Russian prime minister	▮ This information was provided by ▮Primary Subsource's sub-source. The sub-source has been identified as ▮▮▮

*Report Date
**Date Report Provided to FBI by ▮Steele

Report Provided to Journalists, Not FBI
Report Not Provided to Corn

	Report		Information		Corroboration/Analyst Notes
			and his colleagues wanted to have good relations with the US, regardless of who was in power there, and not least so as to be able to travel there in future, either officially or privately. They were openly refusing to cover up for Peskov and others involved in the DNC/Trump operations or to support his counter-attack of allegations against the USG for its alleged hacking of the Russian government and state agencies."		**▇Identifies Primary Subource and subsource▇** ▇ There has been media speculation that Medvedev and Putin have a strained relationship, but this might have started before this alleged operation. [109]
	2016/100 *8/5/16 **9/19/16		"4. According to the first source, close to Ivanov, there had been talk in the Kremlin of Trump being forced to withdraw from the presidential race altogether as a result of recent events, ostensibly on grounds of his psychological state and unsuitability for high office. This might not be so bad for Russia in the circumstances but in the view of the source, it remained largely wishful thinking on the part of those in the regime opposed to Peskov and his "botched" operations, at least for the time being."		▇ This information was provided by ▇Primary Subsource's▇ sub-source. The sub-source has been identified as ▇Primary Subsource's subsource identifies Primary Subource and subsource▇ ▇ On 3 August 2016, the Huffington Post released a blog post titled "The Psychopathology of Donald Trump," which the author examines his psychological state and potential impact if he were to become president. [110]
	2016/101 *8/10/16 **9/19/16		"Head of PA Ivanov assesses the Kremlin intervention in US presidential election and outlines leadership thinking on operational way forward"		
	2016/101 *8/10/16 **9/19/16		"No new leaks envisaged, as too politically risky, but rather further exploitation of (WikiLeaks) material already disseminated to exacerbate divisions"		▇ On 7 October 2016, Wikileaks began dumping John Podesta's e-mails. [111] No reporting was found which would indicate that the Kremlin was aware of or involved with the release of this material.
	2016/101 *8/10/16 **9/19/16		"Educated US youth to be targeted as protest (against Clinton) and swing vote in attempt to turn them over to Trump"		
	2016/101 *8/10/16 **9/19/16		"Russian leadership, including Putin, celebrating perceived success to date splitting US hawks and elite"		
	2016/101 *8/10/16 **9/19/16		"Kremlin engaging with several high profile US players, including Stein, Page and (former DIA Director Michael Flynn), and funding their recent visits to Moscow"		▇ Page admitted to the Washington Post in September 2016 that he briefly spoke with Deputy Prime Minister Arkady Dvorkovich as part of a New Economic School graduation ceremony, where Page was a speaker. [112]

*Report Date
**Date Report Provided to FBI by ▇Steele▇

Report Provided to Journalists. Not FBI
Report Not Provided to Corn

SENATE-FISA2020-001608

	Report		Information		Corroboration/Analyst Notes
					Sequestered by court order

		[113]

    In December 2015 Flynn and Stein were seated at the same table as Putin at RT's 10th anniversary celebration in Moscow. In an interview with *The Washington Post* in August 2016, Flynn admitted that the invitation and payment for his trip came from his speaker's bureau.[114]

    Flynn's trip to Moscow in December 2015 was his second trip to the country. It was the first trip after leaving U.S. government service. Speaking with the FBI, Flynn described receiving a request from Leading Authorities (LAI) to speak on Middle East Issues at RT's 10 Anniversary reception in Moscow. He stated that LAI paid him for the speech and that he did not know from whom LAI received the payment.[115]

    On 16 March 2017, *CNN* published information obtained from the House Oversight Committee detailing a RT's payment to LAI for Flynn's December 2015 speaking engagement in Moscow. The payment covered LAI's fee, LAI's visa expenses, and $33,750 for Flynn's compensation.[116]

    Since the House Oversight Committee obtained documents and an email exchange detailing RT's payment to LAI, other payments to Flynn for speaking engagements have come under media scrutiny. These payments include $11,250 from Volga Dnepr and $11,250 from Kaspersky.[117,118]

    Additionally, news outlets have covered a review of Flynn's financial disclosure submitted on 11 February 2017 and an amended financial

*Report Date
**Date Report Provided to FBI by Steele

Report Provided to Journalists, Not FBI
Report Not Provided to Corn

Report	Information	Corroboration/Analyst Notes
		disclosure submitted on 31 March 2017. Media reporters also allude to the House Oversight Committee's inquiry into Flynn's SF-86s.[119, 120]
2016/101 *8/10/16 **9/19/16	"1. Speaking in confidence to a close colleague in early August 2016, Head of the Russian Presidential Administration (PA), Sergei Ivanov, assessed the impact and results of Kremlin intervention in the US presidential election to date. Although most commentators believed that the Kremlin was behind the leaked DNC/Clinton emails, this remained technically deniable. Therefore the Russians would not risk their position for the time being with the new leaked material, even to a third party like WikiLeaks. Rather the tactics would be to spread rumors and misinformation about the content of what already had been leaked and make up new content."	▓ This information was provided by ▓Primary Subsource's sub-source. The sub-source has been identified as ▓▓▓▓▓▓ Primary Subsource's subsource identifies Primary Subsource and subsou ▓▓▓▓▓▓▓▓▓▓. ▓ In October 2016, Sputnik misattributed a quote from an article to a leaked Wikileaks e-mail from Sidney Blumenthal's account. Sputnik attempted to report that the quote was incriminating in reference to Clinton's time as Secretary of State and her campaign.[121] ▓ On 7 October 2016, Wikileaks began dumping John Podesta's e-mails.[122] No reporting was found which would indicate that the Kremlin was aware of or involved with the release of this material.
2016/101 *8/10/16 **9/19/16	"2. Continuing on this theme, Ivanov said that the audience to be targeted by such operations was the educated youth in America as the PA assessed that there was still a chance they could be persuaded to vote for Republican candidate Donald Trump as a protest against the Washington establishment (in the form of Democratic candidate Hillary Clinton). The hope was that even if she won, as a result of this Clinton in power would be bogged down in working for internal reconciliation in the US, rather than being able to focus on foreign policy which would damage Russia's interests. This also should give President Putin more room for manoeuver in the run-up to Russia's own presidential election in 2018."	▓ This information was provided by ▓Primary Subsource's sub-source. The sub-source has been identified as ▓▓▓ Primary Subsource's subsource identifies Primary Subsource and subsou ▓▓▓▓▓▓▓▓▓▓.
2016/101 *8/10/16 **9/19/16	"3. Ivanov reported that although the Kremlin had underestimated the strength of US media and liberal reaction to the DNC hack and Trump's links to Russia, Putin was	▓ This information was provided by ▓Primary Subsource's sub-source. The sub-source has been identified as ▓▓▓ Primary Subsource's subsource identifies Primary Subsource and subso ▓▓▓▓▓▓▓

*Report Date
**Date Report Provided to FBI by Steele

Report Provided to Journalists, Not FBI
Report Not Provided to Corn

	Report		Information		Corroboration/Analyst Notes
			generally satisfied with the progress of the anti-Clinton operation to date. He recently had had a drink with Putin to mark this. In Ivanov's view, the US had tried to divide the Russian elite with sanctions but failed, whilst they, by contrast, had succeeded in splitting the US hawks inimical to Russia and the Washington elite more generally, half of whom had refused to endorse any presidential candidate as a result of Russian intervention."		▮▮▮ Identifies Primary Subource and subsource ▮▮▮
	▮ 2016/101 *8/10/16 **9/19/16		"4. Speaking separately, also in early August 2016, a Kremlin official involved in US relations commented on aspects of the Russian operation to date. Its goals had been threefold- asking sympathetic US actors how Moscow could help them; gathering relevant intelligence; and creating and disseminating compromising information ('kompromat'). This had involved the Kremlin supporting various US political figures, including funding indirectly their recent visits to Moscow. S/he named a delegation from Lyndon Larouche, presidential candidate Jill Stein of the Green Party; Trump foreign policy adviser Carter Page; and former DIA Director Michael Flynn, in this regard and as successful in terms of perceived outcomes."		▮ Page admitted to the Washington Post in September 2016 that he briefly spoke with Deputy Prime Minister Arkady Dvorkovich as part of a New Economic School graduation ceremony, where Page was a speaker.[123] Sequestered by court order [124] ▮ In December 2015 Flynn and Stein were seated at the same table as Putin in an RT 10th anniversary celebration in Moscow. In an interview in 2016, Flynn admitted that his speaking engagements were funded.[125] ▮ Lyndon LaRouche has a close relationship with Sergey Glazyev since 1994. Glazyev is now a prominent advisor to President Vladimir Putin. Glazyev and LaRouche were connected further through their work with the Duma hearings in June 2001.[126] ▮ In December 2015 Flynn and Stein were seated at the same table as Putin at RT's 10th anniversary celebration in Moscow. In an interview with *The Washington Post* in August 2016, Flynn admitted that the invitation and payment for his trip came from his speaker's bureau.[127]

*Report Date
**Date Report Provided to FBI by ▮Steele▮

Report Provided to Journalists, Not FBI
Report Not Provided to Corn

PRODUCED TO SGJC/SSCI

	Report		Information		Corroboration/Analyst Notes
					☐ Flynn's trip to Moscow in December 2015 was his second trip to the country. It was the first trip after leaving U.S. government service. Speaking with the FBI, Flynn described receiving a request from Leading Authorities (LAI) to speak on Middle East Issues at RT's 10 Anniversary reception in Moscow. He stated that LAI paid him for the speech and that he did not know from whom LAI received the payment.[128]
					☐ On 16 March 2017, *CNN* published information obtained from the House Oversight Committee detailing a RT's payment to LAI for Flynn's December 2015 speaking engagement in Moscow. The payment covered LAI's fee, LAI's visa expenses, and $33,750 for Flynn's compensation.[129]
					☐ Since the House Oversight Committee obtained documents and an email exchange detailing RT's payment to LAI, other payments to Flynn for speaking engagements have come under media scrutiny. These payments include $11,250 from Volgna Dnepr and $11,250 from Kaspersky.[130,131]
					☐ Additionally, news outlets have covered a review of Flynn's financial disclosure submitted on 11 February 2017 and an amended financial disclosure submitted on 31 March 2017. Media reporters also allude to the House Oversight Committee's inquiry into Flynn's SF-86s.[132, 133]
☐	2016/102 *8/10/16 **9/19/16	☐	"Trump campaign insider reports recent DNC email leaks were aimed at switching Sanders (protest) voters away from Clinton and over to Trump"		
☐	2016/102 *8/10/16 **9/19/16	☐	"Admits Republican campaign underestimated resulting negative reaction from US liberals, elite, and media and forced to change course as result"		
☐	2016/102 *8/10/16 **9/19/16	☐	"Need now to turn tables on Clinton's use of Putin as bogeyman in election, although some resentment at Russian president's perceived attempt to undermine USG and system over and above swinging presidential election"		☐ As of late July 2016, reports of Democrats and Clinton using the "Russia Card" began after the DNC hacking and e-mail leak in mainstream U.S media.[134]

*Report Date
**Date Report Provided to FBI by Steele

Report Provided to Journalists, Not FBI
Report Not Provided to Corn

	Report		Information		Corroboration/Analyst Notes
					▮ As of September 2016, reports begin in Sputnik about Hillary Clinton using the "Russia Card" against Trump. [135]
▮	2016/102 *8/10/16 **9/19/16	▮	"1. Speaking in confidence on 9 August 2016, an ethnic Russian associate of Republican US presidential candidate Donald Trump discussed the reaction inside his camp, and revised tactics therein resulting from recent negative publicity concerning Moscow's clandestine involvement in the campaign. Trump's associate reported that the aim of leaking DNC emails to WikiLeaks during the Democratic National Convention had been to swing supporters of Bernie Sanders away from Hillary Clinton and across to Trump. These voters were perceived as activist and anti-status quo and anti-establishment and in that regard sharing many features with the Trump campaign, including a visceral dislike of Hillary Clinton. This objective had been conceived and promoted, inter alia, by Trump's foreign policy adviser Carter Page who had discussed it directly with the ethnic Russian associate."		
▮	2016/102 *8/10/16 **9/19/16	▮	"2. Continuing on this theme, the ethnic Russian associate of Trump assessed that the problem was that the Trump campaign had underestimated the strength of the negative reaction from liberals and especially the conservative elite to Russian interference. This was forcing a rethink and a likely change of tactics. The main objective in the short term was to check Democratic candidate Hillary Clinton's successful exploitation of the Putin as bogeyman/Russian interference story to tarnish Trump and bolster her own (patriotic) credentials. The Trump campaign was focusing on tapping into support in the American television media to achieve this, as they reckoned this resource had been underused by them to date."	▮	As of late July 2016, reports of Democrats and Clinton using the "Russia Card" began after the DNC hacking and e-mail leak in mainstream U.S media. [136] ▮ As of September 2016, reports begin in Sputnik about Hillary Clinton using the "Russia Card" against Trump. [137]
▮	2016/102 *8/10/16 **9/19/16	▮	"3. However, Trump's associate also admitted that there was a fair amount of anger and resentment within the Republican candidate's team at what was perceived by Putin as going beyond the objective of weakening Clinton and bolstering		

*Report Date
**Date Report Provided to FBI by Steele

Report Provided to Journalists, Not FBI
Report Not Provided to Corn

Report	Information	Corroboration/Analyst Notes
	Trump, by attempting to exploit the situation to undermine the US government and democratic system more generally. It was unclear at present how this aspect of the situation would play out in the weeks to come.	
2016/105 *8/22/16	"Ex-Ukrainian President YANUKOVYCH confides directly to Putin that he authorized kick-back payments to Manafort, as alleged in western media. Assures Russian President however there is no documentary evidence/trail"	The first story referencing secret payments discovered on a ledger in Ukraine that shows that Manafort was owed $12 million by the Ukraine government was the New York Times on 14 August 2016.[138] Other Agency Information [139] Sensitive FBI Information [140]
2016/105 *8/22/16	"Putin and Russian leadership remain worried however and skeptical that Yanukovych has fully covered the traces of these payments to Trump's former campaign manager"	Other Agency Information [141] Sources and Methods
2016/105 *8/22/16	"[REDACTED] recent meetings between President Putin and ex-President Yanukovych of Ukraine. This had been held in secret on 15 August near Volgograd, Russia and the western media revelations about Manafort and Ukraine had featured prominently on the agenda."	Unable to verify meeting between Putin and Yanukovych or the date/place of meeting as of 11/14/2016. Erdogan and Putin Meeting – 09 August 2016 (St. Petersburg, Russia) Azeri and Iranian Leaders Meeting – 08 August 2016 (Baku, Azerbaijan) No relevant information found regarding search terms "Yanukovich" and "Volgograd."
2016/105 *8/22/16	"Yanukovych had confided in Putin that he did authorize and order substantial kick-back payments to Manafort as alleged but sought to reassure him that there was no documentary trail left behind which could provide clear evidence of this."	The first story referencing secret payments discovered on a ledger in Ukraine that shows that Manafort was owed $12 million by the Ukraine government was the New York Times on 14 August 2016.[142] Other Agency Information [143]

*Report Date
**Date Report Provided to FBI by Steele

Report Provided to Journalists, Not FBI
Report Not Provided to Corn

PRODUCED TO SJC/SSCI

	Report		Information		Corroboration/Analyst Notes
					Sensitive FBI Information [144]
	2016/105 *8/22/16		"Given Yanukovych's (unimpressive) record in covering up his own corrupt tracks in the past, Putin and others in the Russian leadership were skeptical about the ex-Ukrainian president's reassurance on this as relating to Manafort. They therefore still feared the scandal had legs, especially as Manafort had been commercially active in Ukraine right up to the time (in March 2016) when he joined Trump's campaign team. For them it therefore remained a point of potentially political vulnerability and embarrassment."		The first story referencing secret payments discovered on a ledger in Ukraine that shows that Manafort was owed $12 million by the Ukraine government was the New York Times on 14 August 2016. [145]
					Other Agency Information [146]
					Sensitive FBI Information [147]
	2016/111 *9/14/16		"Kremlin orders senior staff to remain silent in media and private on allegations of Russian interference in US presidential campaign"		Other Agency Information
					Other Agency Information [149]
	2016/111 *9/14/16		"[REDACTED] Ivanov sacked as Head of Administration on account of giving Putin poor advice on issue."		A program summary of Rossiya 1 TV indicates that Ivanov was sacked as Head of Administration on 12 August 2016, one month and two days after Steele reporting. [150] Kremlin.ru reporting shows a dialogue between Putin, Ivanov, and Vaino, with Putin thanking Ivanov for his excellent service. Putin then tells Ivanov that Putin granted Ivanov Ivanov's wish to be in the position no longer than four years. Putin then tells Vaino that Ivanov recommended Vaino and that Putin agreed. Vaino thanks both of them. Ivanov then praises Vaino for the work he did for Ivanov. [151]

*Report Date
**Date Report Provided to FBI by Steele

Report Provided to Journalists, Not FBI
Report Not Provided to Corn

PRODUCED TO SJC/SSCI

Report	Information	Corroboration/Analyst Notes
		Other Agency Information
2016/111 *9/14/16	"Vaino selected as his replacement partly because he was not involved in pro-Trump, anti-Clinton operation/s"	Other Agency Information [153]
		Kremlin.ru reporting shows a dialogue between Putin, Ivanov, and Vaino, with Putin thanking Ivanov for his excellent service. Putin then tells Ivanov that Putin granted Ivanov Ivanov's wish to be in the position no longer than four years. Putin then tells Vaino that Ivanov recommended Vaino and that Putin agreed. Vaino thanks both of them. Ivanov then praises Vaino for the work he did for Ivanov.[154]
		Other Agency Information

*Report Date
**Date Report Provided to FBI by Steele

Report Provided to Journalists, Not FBI
Report Not Provided to Corn

SENATE-FISA2020-001616

	Report		Information		Corroboration/Analyst Notes	
					▉ Other Agency Information ▉	
					[155]	
▉	2016/111 *9/14/16	▉	"Russians do have further 'kompromat' on Clinton (e-mails) and considering disseminating it after Duma (legislative elections) in late September. Presidential spokesman Peskov continues to lead on this"		▉ Other Agency Information ▉	
					[156]	
					▉ It is unclear whether the Russians had further kompromat on Clinton, although Wikileaks disseminated emails both before and after the Duma elections with the Podesta emails starting on 7 October 2016. It is also unclear if Peskov has the lead on any dissemination.	
▉	2016/111 *9/14/16	▉	"However, equally important is Kremlin objective to shift policy consensus favorably to Russia in US post-Obama whoever wins."		▉ In Putin's Valdai speech on 27 October 2016, he specifically says that Russia is not interfering with the US election and has "no intention of attacking anyone" despite evidence on the contrary. He also states that "I would like to have such a propaganda machine here in Russia... of the likes of CNN, BBC, and others. We simply do not have this capability yet."	
					▉ In a 16 October 2016 speech in India, Putin addressed reporters and said that Moscow would welcome any US leader who is willing to work with Russia.[157]	
▉	2016/111 *9/14/16	▉	"Both presidential candidates' opposition to TPP and TTIP viewed as a result in this respect"	▉ Clinton TPP		▉ Trump TPP
				08 September 2010 – CFR Speech "We're pursuing a regional agreement with the nations of the Trans-Pacific Partnership..."[158]		22 April 2015 – Tweet "The TPP is an attack on America's businesses"[169]
						May 2015 – Daily Caller Criticism of TPP[170]
				09 March 2011 – APEC Forum "The US is also making important progress on the TPP..."[159]		05 October 2015 – Tweet "TPP is a terrible deal"[171]

*Report Date
**Date Report Provided to FBI by ▉Steele▉

Report Provided to Journalists, Not FBI
Report Not Provided to Corn

▮ Report	▮ Information	▮ Corroboration/Analyst Notes	
		08 July 2012 – Conversation with a Japanese Official "The US welcomes Japan's interest in the TPP..." [160]	10 November 2015 – Debate "The TPP is a horrible deal" [172]
		05 November 2012 – Remarks in Australia "This TPP sets the gold standard in trade agreements" [161]	14 March 2016 – op-ed "TPP is the biggest betrayal in a long line of betrayals were politicians have sold out U.S. workers." [173]
		13 November 2013 – Wikileaks released TPP Intellectual Property Rights Chapter[162]	
		July 2014 – Hard Choices Memoir "become the economic pillar of our strategy in Asia" [163]	28 June 2016 – "The TPP is another disaster done and pushed by special interests" [174]
		22 May 2015 – NH Press Conference "I want to judge this when I see exactly what exactly is in it and whether or not I think it meets my standards" [164]	TTIP Neither candidate has issued a concrete stance on TTIP, although with their opposition, it is assumed they are also critical of TTIP. [175]
		08 October 2015 – "I am not in favor of what I have learned about it" [165]	
		October 2016 – Wikileaks released Podesta emails showing Clinton support for TPP in June 2015[166]	

*Report Date
**Date Report Provided to FBI by Steele

Report Provided to Journalists, Not FBI
Report Not Provided to Corn

SENATE-FISA2020-001618

	Report		Information		Corroboration/Analyst Notes
					23 October 2016 – Leaked memo from Wikileaks shows Soros and his Open Society Foundation as coming out against the TPP and criticizing the Obama administration for undermining democracy in Malaysia.[167]
					TTIP Neither candidate has issued a concrete stance on TTIP, although with their opposition, it is assumed they are also critical of TTIP.[168]
					According to Wikileaks emails, the shift in Clinton's support was due to getting support from unions.[176]
	2016/111 *9/14/16		"Senior Russian diplomat withdrawn from Washington embassy on account of potential exposure in US presidential election operation/s"		The name Mikhail Kulagin not found in FBI Sources and Methods that could be the senior diplomat as of 14 November 2016. It is believed a misspelling of Mikhail Aleksandrovich Kalugin, a Russian diplomat.
					Sensitive FBI Information [177]
	2016/111 *9/14/16		"[REDACTED] Putin had been receiving conflicting advice on interfering from three separate and expert groups." "On one side had been the Russian ambassador to the US, Sergei Kislyak, and the Ministry of Foreign Affairs, together with an independent and informal network run by presidential foreign policy advisor, Yuri Ushakov (Kislyak's predecessor in Washington) who had urged caution and the potential negative impact on Russia from the operation/s."		Other Agency Information [178] Other Agency Information

*Report Date
**Date Report Provided to FBI by Steele

Report Provided to Journalists, Not FBI
Report Not Provided to Corn

▮ Report	▮ Information	Corroboration/Analyst Notes
		Other Agency Information [179]
		Other Agency Information [180]
		Other Agency Information [81]
		Other Agency Information [182]
		Other Agency Information [183]
		Other Agency Information
▮ 2016/111 *9/14/16	▮ "On the other side was former PA Head, Sergei Ivanov, backed by Russian Foreign Intelligence (SVR) , who had advised Putin that the pro-Trump, anti-Clinton operation/s would be both effective and plausibly deniable with little blowback."	Other Agency Information [184]

*Report Date
**Date Report Provided to FBI by Steele

Report Provided to Journalists, Not FBI
Report Not Provided to Corn

SENATE-FISA2020-001620

	Report		Information		Corroboration/Analyst Notes
▪	2016/111 *9/14/16	▪	"The first group/s had been proven right and this had been the catalyst in Putin's decision to sack Ivanov (unexpectedly) as PA Head in August."	▪	Kremlin.ru reporting shows a dialogue between Putin, Ivanov, and Vaino, with Putin thanking Ivanov for his excellent service. Putin then tells Ivanov that Putin granted Ivanov Ivanov's wish to be in the position no longer than four years. Putin then tells Vaino that Ivanov recommended Vaino and that Putin agreed. Vaino thanks both of them. Ivanov then praises Vaino for the work he did for Ivanov.[185] Other Agency Information [186]
▪	2016/111 *9/14/16	▪	"His successor, Anton Vaino, had been selected for the job partly because he had not been involved in the US presidential election operation/s."	▪	Kremlin.ru reporting shows a dialogue between Putin, Ivanov, and Vaino, with Putin thanking Ivanov for his excellent service. Putin then tells Ivanov that Putin granted Ivanov Ivanov's wish to be in the position no longer than four years. Putin then tells Vaino that Ivanov recommended Vaino and that Putin agreed. Vaino thanks both of them. Ivanov then praises Vaino for the work he did for Ivanov.[187] Other Agency Information

*Report Date
**Date Report Provided to FBI by Steele

Report Provided to Journalists, Not FBI
Report Not Provided to Corn

SENATE-FISA2020-001621

	Report		Information		Corroboration/Analyst Notes
					Other Agency Information ██████████████████████ [188]
	2016/111 *9/14/16		"[REDACTED] Kremlin had further 'kompromat' on candidate Clinton and had been considering releasing this via "plausibly deniable" channels"		A twitter feed search revealed that on 7 October 2016 Wikileaks began publishing Podesta's emails [189] ████ If referring to Wikileaks, this would be confirmed as of 14 November 2016.
	2016/111 *9/14/16		"after the Duma (legislative) elections were out of the way in mid-September."		The Duma elections occurred on 18 September 2016 and saw the ruling pro-Kremlin party United Russia win 343 out of 450 seats in the new State Duma. [190]
	2016/111 *9/14/16		"There was however a growing train of thought and associated lobby, arguing that the Russian could still make candidate Clinton look "weak and stupid" by provoking her into railing against Putin and Russia without the need to release more of her e-mails."		As of late July 2016, reports of Democrats and Clinton using the "Russia Card" began after the DNC hacking and e-mail leak in mainstream U.S media. [191] ████) As of September 2016, reports begin in Sputnik about Hillary Clinton using the "Russia Card" against Trump. [192]
	2016/111 *9/14/16		"Presidential Spokesman, Dmitriy Peskov remained a key figure in the operation, although any final decision on dissemination of further material would be taken by Putin himself."		**Other Agency Information** ██████████████████████ [193]
	2016/111 *9/14/16		"[REDACTED] Moscow's intervention in the US presidential election campaign was the objective of shifting the US political consensus in Russia's perceived interests regardless of who won. It basically comprised of pushing candidate Clinton away from President Obama's policies"		In a 16 October 2016 speech in India, Putin addressed reporters and said that Moscow would welcome any US leader who is willing to work with Russia. [194]

*Report Date
**Date Report Provided to FBI by Steele

Report Provided to Journalists, Not FBI
Report Not Provided to Corn

PRODUCED TO SJC/SSCI

PRODUCED TO SJC/SSCI

Report	Information	Corroboration/Analyst Notes	
2016/111 *9/14/16	"The best example of this was that both candidates now openly opposed the draft trade agreements, TPP and TTIP, which were assessed by Moscow as detrimental to Russian interests."	Clinton TPP 08 September 2010 – CFR Speech "We're pursuing a regional agreement with the nations of the Trans-Pacific Partnership..."[195] 09 March 2011 – APEC Forum "The US is also making important progress on the TPP..."[196] 08 July 2012 – Conversation with a Japanese Official "The US welcomes Japan's interest in the TPP..."[197] 05 November 2012 – Remarks in Australia "This TPP sets the gold standard in trade agreements"[198] 13 November 2013 – Wikileaks released TPP Intellectual Property Rights Chapter[199] July 2014 – Hard Choices Memoir "become the economic pillar of our strategy in Asia"[200] 22 May 2015 – NH Press Conference "I want to judge this when I see exactly what exactly	Trump TPP 22 April 2015 – Tweet "The TPP is an attack on America's businesses"[206] May 2015 – Daily Caller Criticism of TPP[207] 05 October 2015 – Tweet "TPP is a terrible deal"[208] 10 November 2015 – Debate "The TPP is a horrible deal"[209] 14 March 2016 – op-ed "TPP is the biggest betrayal in a long line of betrayals were politicians have sold out U.S. workers."[210] 28 June 2016 – "The TPP is another disaster done and pushed by special interests"[211] TTIP Neither candidate has issued a concrete stance on TTIP, although with their opposition, it is assumed they are also critical of TTIP.[212]

*Report Date
**Date Report Provided to FBI by Steele

Report Provided to Journalists, Not FBI
Report Not Provided to Corn

SENATE-FISA2020-001623

	Report		Information		Corroboration/Analyst Notes	
					is in it and whether or not I think it meets my standards" [201]	
					08 October 2015 – "I am not in favor of what I have learned about it" [202]	
					October 2016 – Wikileaks released Podesta emails showing Clinton support for TPP in June 2015 [203]	
					23 October 2016 – Leaked memo from Wikileaks shows Soros and his Open Society Foundation as coming out against the TPP and criticizing the Obama administration for undermining democracy in Malaysia. [204]	
					TTIP Neither candidate has issued a concrete stance on TTIP, although with their opposition, it is assumed they are also critical of TTIP. [205]	
					▮▮▮▮) According to Wikileaks emails, the shift in Clinton's support was due to getting support from unions. [213]	
	2016/111 *9/14/16		"Other issues where the Kremlin was looking to shift the US policy consensus were Ukraine and Syria. Overall however, the presidential election was considering still to be too close to call."			
	2016/111 *9/14/16		"[REDACTED] a leading Russian diplomat, Mikhail Kulagin, [redacted] withdrawn from Washington at short notice because		This information was provided by Primary Subsource. Primary Subsource **Primary Subsource Identifying**	

*Report Date
**Date Report Provided to FBI by Steele

Report Provided to Journalists, Not FBI
Report Not Provided to Corn

	Report		Information	Corroboration/Analyst Notes
			Moscow feared his heavy involvement in the US presidential election operation, including the so-called veterans' pensions ruse (reported previously), would be exposed in the media there."	**Primary Subsource Identifying** ▮▮▮ **Sources and Methods** ▮▮▮ It is believed a misspelling of Mikhail Aleksandrovich Kalugin, a Russian diplomat. **Sensitive FBI Information** ▮▮▮ [214]
	2016/111 *9/14/16		"His replacement, Andrei Bondarev however was clean in this regard."	**Sources and Methods** [215] **Sensitive FBI Information** ▮▮▮ [216]
	2016/112 *9/14/16		"[REDACTED] Significant favors continue to be done in both directions and Fridman and Aven still giving informal advice to Putin, especially on the US"	According to Sydney's Morning Herald, Fridman, Russia's second richest man employs Pyotr Aven, an economist who worked with Putin in St. Petersburg. Aven helped Putin beat corruption charges and Aven and Fridman have been known to be in "Moscow's corridors of power". [217]

*Report Date
**Date Report Provided to FBI by ▮Steele▮

Report Provided to Journalists, Not FBI
Report Not Provided to Corn

PRODUCED TO SJC/SSCI

▮ Report	▮ Information	▮ Corroboration/Analyst Notes
		▮ The man who authored Trump's first big foreign policy speech, Richard Burt, sits on Alfa's (Fridman's company) senior advisory board.[218] ▮ An Interfax article September 2016 and Fridman and Aven's names show's an Interfax article about the removal of board member Slobodin.[219] ▮Other Agency Information ▮▮▮ [220] ▮Other Agency Information ▮▮▮ [221] ▮▮▮ While there is history, there does not seem to be any concrete, current information as of 14 November 2016.
▮ 2016/112 *9/14/16	▮ "Key intermediary in Putin-Alpha relationship identified as Oleg Govorun, currently head of a presidential administration department but throughout the 1990s, the Alpha executive who delivered illicit cash directly to Putin"	▮ Govorun was vice-president of Alfa-Bank and deputy head of the bank's directorate for communications with state bodies.[222] ▮▮▮ As of 09 September 2016, Govorun was the head of the Directorate for Social and Economic Relations, with the Commonwealth of Independent States, South Ossetia, and Abkhazia.[223]
▮ 2016/112 *9/14/16	▮ "Putin personally unbothered about Alpha's current lack of investment in Russia but under pressure from colleagues over this and able to exploit it as lever over Alpha interlocutors"	▮ On 25 November 2014, Putin signed a law that cracks down on offshore tax sheltering, which would impact Alfa Group Consortium.[224] ▮ On 06 February 2015, Sputnik published "Everyone's a winner as Russian Banks and European Savers team up." The public sentiment does not seem to be against Alfa.[225]

*Report Date
**Date Report Provided to FBI by Steele

Report Provided to Journalists, Not FBI
Report Not Provided to Corn

	Report		Information		Corroboration/Analyst Notes
	2016/112 *9/14/16		"[REDACTED] although they had had their ups and downs, the leading figures in Alpha currently [redacted] on very good terms with Putin."		**Other Agency Information**
					According to ▮ reporting from 14 September 2016, Russian corruption cases were being used to target (among others) Fridman.[227]
	2016/112 *9/14/16		"Significant favors continued to be done in both directions, primarily political ones for Putin and business/legal ones for Alfa." "Also, Fridman and Aven continued to give informal advice to Putin on foreign policy, and especially about the US where he distrusted advice being given to him by officials."		**Other Agency Information** [228]
	2016/112 *9/14/16		"Although Fridman recently had met directly with Putin in Russia, much of the dialogue and business between them was mediated through a senior presidential administration official, Oleg Govorun, who currently headed the department therein responsible for Social Co-operation with the CIS."		**Other Agency Information** [229] **Other Agency Information** [230] Govorun was formerly Vice President of the Joint-Stock Company.[231]
	2016/112 *9/14/16		"Govorun was trusted by Putin and recently had accompanied him to Uzbekistan to pay respects at the tomb of former president Karimov. [REDACTED] during the 1990s Govorun had been Head of Government Relations at Alpha Group and in reality, the "driver" and "bag carrier" used by		Govorun was reprimanded by Putin personally in October 2012 and resigned from his post as Regional Development Minister.[232] According to Sputnik, a busy schedule precluded Putin's visit to Memorial Service for Karimov on 03 September 2016.[233]

*Report Date
**Date Report Provided to FBI by Steele

Report Provided to Journalists, Not FBI
Report Not Provided to Corn

PRODUCED TO SIC/SSCI

PRODUCED TO SJC/SSCI

Report	Information	Corroboration/Analyst Notes
	Fridman and Aven to deliver large amounts of illicit cash to the Russian president, at that time deputy Mayor of St. Petersburg."	According to India Express, Putin laid flowers at Karimov's grave on 06 September 2016.[234] No information about Govorun's role in the 90's could be found outside of his role as VP of Alfa Bank.[235]
2016/112 *9/14/16	"Given that the continuing sensitivity of the Putin-Alpha relationship, and need for plausible deniability, much of the contact between them was now indirect and entrusted to the relatively low profile Govorun."	No information about Govorun's role in the 90's could be found outside of his role as VP of Alfa Bank.[236]
2016/112 *9/14/16	"[REDACTED] Alfa held 'kompromat' on Putin and his corrupt business activities form the 1990s whilst although not personally overly bothered by Alpha's failure to reinvest the proceeds of its TNK oil company sale into the Russian economy since, the Russian president was able to use pressure on this count from senior Kremlin colleagues as a lever on Fridman and Aven to make them do his political bidding."	According to Sputnik, a consortium of Alfa Access, and Renova made $28 billion dollars on the deal that was signed on 12 December 2012. No open source criticism was found of Alfa regarding the TNK deal.[237]
2016/113 *09/14/16	1. Speaking to a trusted compatriot in September 2016, two well-placed sources based in St Petersburg, one in the political/business elite and the other involved in the local services and tourist industry, commented on Republican US presidential candidate Donald TRUMP's prior activities in the city.	
2016/113 *09/14/16	2. Both knew TRUMP had visited St Petersburg on several occasions in the past and had been interested in doing business deals there involving real estate. The local business/political elite figure reported that TRUMP had paid bribes there to further his interests but very discreetly and only through affiliated companies, making it very hard to prove. The local services industry source reported that TRUMP had participated in sex parties in the city too, but that all direct witnesses to this recently had been "silenced" i.e. bribed or coerced to disappear.	This information was provided by Primary Subsource's sub-source. The sub-source was identified as Primary Subsource's subsource Identifying Primary Subsource and Subsource This information could have also been provided by another sub-source. The sub-source was identified as Primary Subsource's subsource Identifying Primary Subsource and Subsource

*Report Date
**Date Report Provided to FBI by Steele

Report Provided to Journalists, Not FBI
Report Not Provided to Corn

Report	Information	Corroboration/Analyst Notes
▮ 2016/113 *09/14/16	▮ 3. The two St Petersburg figures cited believed an Azeri business figure, Araz AGALAROV (with offices in Baku and London) had been closely involved with TRUMP in Russia and would know most of the details of what the Republican presidential candidate had got up to there.	▮ This information was provided by ▮Primary Subsource's sub-source. The sub-source was identified as ▮Primary Subsource's subsource Identifying Primary Subsource and Subsource ▮ ▮ This information could have also been provided by another ▮Primary Subsource sub-source. The sub-source was identified as ▮Primary Subsource's subsource Identifying Primary Subsource and Subsource ▮
▮ Winer **10/19/16	▮ "...a military wing of the GRU was overseeing [a] hacking operation in the [United States]."	▮ This report was shared by Individual 1 who is a ▮Identifies in ▮ .238 ▮ The GRU role in hacking has been established in open source reporting; however this is the only report that mentions the GRU overseeing the hacking operation.
▮ Winer **10/19/16	▮ "...a division of the FSB [of which the FSB interlocutor is part] that thinks the existence of a 'pervasive' and 'sophisticated' intelligence operation focusing on pivotal US personalities is widely known, specifically the Donald Trump operation."	Other Agency Information ▮ ▮ Other than open source speculation, the only reporting that mentions this is the Steele Reporting from 5 July 2016 and 2 August 2016.] ▮ This report was shared by Individual 1 who is a ▮Identifies in ▮

*Report Date
**Date Report Provided to FBI by Steele

Report Provided to Journalists, Not FBI
Report Not Provided to Corn

■ Report	■ Information	■ Corroboration/Analyst Notes
		Other Agency Information
■ Winer **10/19/16	■ "...the Trump operation was an 'open secret' in Putin's government circles."	This report was shared by Individual 1 who is a ▮▮▮▮ ▮▮▮▮▮▮▮▮▮▮ 240
		▮▮▮ There is no reference to "open secret" in previous reporting, however the prior Steele reporting from 5 and 25 July 2016, 29 August 2016, and 19 October 2016 indicated several individuals in the Russian government were aware of the operation.
■ Winer **10/19/16	■ "...Trump was filmed twice in Moscow in November 2013 during the Miss Universe pageant."	■ The pageant took place on 9 November 2013 in Moscow, Russia.[241]
		This report was shared by Individual 1 who is a ▮▮▮▮ ▮▮▮▮▮▮▮▮▮▮ 242
■ Winer **10/19/16	■ "[one of the filming] occurred in the Presidential Suite of the Ritz Carlton Hotel."	This report was shared by Individual 1 who is a ▮▮▮▮ ▮▮▮▮▮▮▮▮▮▮
		▮▮▮ On 14 January 2017, a CHS reported to FBI ▮▮▮▮▮ that Individual 1 was attempting to provide information about a Individual 2 who was allegedly willing to defect to the U.S. The Individual 2 claimed to have compromising tapes on President Donald Trump.[244] *[Analyst Note: It is unknown if the tapes mentioned in this reporting are the same tapes mentioned in report 80. The only similar information is the use of "tapes"* Identifies ▮▮▮▮

*Report Date
**Date Report Provided to FBI by Steele

Report Provided to Journalists, Not FBI
Report Not Provided to Corn

■ Report	■ Information	■ Corroboration/Analyst Notes
		■ There is no confirmation that Trump stayed here. There is no "Presidential Suite" currently listed, though they do have the Moscow Suite, Ritz-Carlton Suite, Carlton Suite, Teverskaya Suite, and the Executive Suite.[245] There is mention of the Presidential suite in a press release from 2015.[246] ■ In 2009 President Obama stayed in the Presidential suite at the Ritz-Carlton Hotel in Moscow which is described as a five room kremlin view luxury suite with huge panoramic windows.[247] **Other Agency Information** ██████████████████████████[248]
■ Winer **10/19/16	■ "[one of the filming took place] at the Crocus shopping mall where the pageant was held"	■ The pageant was held at the Crocus International Exhibition Center which does have shops and is attached to a hotel (Aquarium Hotel).[249] This report was shared by Individual 1 who is a ███████ ████████████████[250]
■ Winer **10/19/16	■ "...there is a special complex for distinguished guests in the Crocus Complex with all the amenities including a pool..."	This report was shared by Individual 1 who is a ███████ ████████████████[251] ■ The Crocus Group has several buildings in Moscow, including the Crocus International Exhibition Center, and The Crocus City Hall (concert venue), and the Aquarium Hotel. Both venues are large and appear to have several amenities; however, neither a pool nor a "special complex for distinguished guests" is listed."[252]

*Report Date
**Date Report Provided to FBI by Steele

Report Provided to Journalists, Not FBI
Report Not Provided to Corn

	Report		Information		Corroboration/Analyst Notes
▮	Winer **10/19/16	▮	"This [Crocus] complex is owned by the Agalarov family"	▮	This report was shared by **Individual 1** who is a ▮ ▮ [253] ▮ The Crocus Group is owned and controlled by the Agalarov family.[254]
▮	Winer **10/19/16	▮	"[Trump] was also filmed in St. Petersburg"	▮	This report was shared by **Individual 1** who is a ▮ [55] ▮ Trump was in St. Petersburg in 1987 working on a real-estate deal, and in 2008 Trump claimed to have been to Russia six times in 18 months. Though he did not mention St. Petersburg, the real estate deal he was negotiating included a hotel in St. Petersburg.[256,257]
▮	Winer **10/19/16	▮	"[The] first FSB-generated payment [$10 million] to Trump took place in Baku at the presidential palace, which Trump took personally."	▮	This report was shared by **Individual 1** who is a ▮ ▮ There doesn't appear to be any record of Trump visiting Baku or the presidential palace, though he may have traveled there at some point during the negotiations of the Trump Tower project.[259]
▮	Winer **10/19/16	▮	"[The] next payment...went to [Trump's] daughter Ivanka"	▮	This report was shared by **Individual 1** who is ▮ [260]

*Report Date
Date Report Provided to FBI by **Steele

Report Provided to Journalists, Not FBI
Report Not Provided to Corn

Report	Information	Corroboration/Analyst Notes
		Ivanka was took the lead on the Trump Tower project in Baku from its inception and she appears to have traveled there in 2014 and 2015.[261]
Winer **10/19/16	"The FSB money was originally passed through Aras Agalarov...who served as a liaison between Trump and Putin"	This report was shared by Individual 1 who is a ▓▓▓ [262]
		Trump does have a relationship with the Agalarov family, dating back to at least 2013. The Agalarov family has been a awarded numerous commercial contracts in Russia and in 2013, Putin himself awarded Aras Agalarov with the Russian medal of honor.[263]
Winer **10/19/16	"Anar Mammadov, the son of Azerbaijan Transport Minister Ziya Mammadov, was also involved"	This report was shared by Individual 1 who is a ▓▓▓ [264]
		Anar Mammadov is the billionaire son of Ziya Mammadov, Azerbaijan's transportation minister.[265]
Winer **10/19/16	"[They used the presidential palace in Baku] because Aras Agalarov's son, Emin, is married to Leyla Aliyeva, the daughter of Azerbaijan's president Ilham Aliyev."	This report was shared by Individual 1 who is a ▓▓▓ [266]
		Leyla Aliyeva was married to Emin Agalarov in 2013, however, they divorced in 2015. She is the daughter of the current president of Azerbaijan, who took office in 2003.[267,268]
Winer **10/19/16	"[Emin] got Trump to perform in a music video"	This report was shared by Individual 1 who is ▓▓▓

*Report Date
**Date Report Provided to FBI by Steele

Report Provided to Journalists, Not FBI
Report Not Provided to Corn

PRODUCED TO SSCI/CSSCI

■ Report	■ Information	■ Corroboration/Analyst Notes
		Identifies Individual 1 ████████████████████ ■ ████ .269 ■ On 20 November 2013, Trump appeared in Emin Agalarov's video titled "In Another Life"[270]
■ Winer **10/19/16	■ "[Following acceptance of the $10 million, which Trump took personally in Baku] Trump promised to support Aliyev politically, and also promised to organize a Congressional trip to Baku."	███████ This report was shared by Individual 1 who is Identifies Indi ████████████████████████████ ████████████████████████████ ████████████████████████████ ████ .271 ■ Trump is not on record for saying positive things about President Aliyev; however he was in negotiations with Anar Mammadov to use the Trump name for a hotel and condo tower in Baku. The Mammadov family is very closely tied to Aliyev. [272] ■ There is no record of Trump personally organizing a Congressional Delegation (CODEL) visit to Baku, but there have been at least two CODEL visits came under public scrutiny. The first occurred in 2013, when 10 members of Congress and 32 of their staff visited Baku and the trip was paid for by the State Oil Company of the Azerbaijan Republic (SOCAR). This trip included several thousand dollars in illegal gifts, and was ultimately investigated by the Office of Congressional Ethics. [273] ■ The second CODEL visit that was scrutinized was one that occurred on 14 November 2014, when four prominent US Senators and several congressmen attended the Azerbaijan American Alliance third annual gala dinner. [274]
■ 2016/130 *10/12/2016 **10/19/2016	■████ "...a degree of buyer's remorse was setting in among Russian leaders concerning TRUMP. PUTIN and his colleagues were surprised and disappointed that leaks of Democratic candidate Hillary CLINTON's hacked e-mails had not had great impact on the campaign."	

*Report Date
**Date Report Provided to FBI by Steele

Report Provided to Journalists, Not FBI
Report Not Provided to Corn

	Report		Information		Corroboration/Analyst Notes
■	2016/130 *10/12/2016 **10/19/2016	■	"...a stream of further hacked CLINTON material already had been injected by the Kremlin into compliant western media outlets like Wikileaks, which remained at least "plausibly deniable", so the stream of these would continue through October and up to the election."		
■	2016/130 *10/12/2016 **10/19/2016	■	"...understood that the best material the Russians had already was out and there were no real game-changers to come."		
■	2016/130 *10/12/2016 **10/19/2016	■	"...PUTIN was angry at his subordinate's "over-promising" on the Republican presidential candidate, both in terms of his chances and reliability and being able to cover and/or contain the US backlash over Kremlin interference."		
■	2016/130 *10/12/2016 **10/19/2016	■	"...Foreign Minister LAVROV could be the next one to go."		
■	2016/130 *10/12/2016 **10/19/2016	■	"...Russia needed to upset the liberal international status quo, including on Ukraine-related sanctions, which was seriously disadvantaging the country."		
■	2016/130 *10/12/2016 **10/19/2016	■	"TRUMP was viewed as divisive in disrupting the whole US political system; anti-Establishment; and a pragmatist with whom they could do business."	■ ■	reporting corroborates that Russia believes Trump would make a good president and that positive relations can be formed with a Trump administration.[275,276]
■	2016/130 *10/12/2016 **10/19/2016	■	"As the TRUMP support operation had gained momentum, control of it had passed from the MFA to the FSB and then into the presidential administration where it remained, a reflection of its growing significance over time."		Sensitive FBI Information [277,278]
■	2016/130 *10/12/2016 **10/19/2016	■	"There was still a view in the Kremlin that TRUMP would continue as a (divisive) political force even if he lost the presidency and may run for and be elected to another public office."		
■	2016/132 *10/13/2016 **10/19/2016	■	"...PUTIN now regretted Moscow's operation to interfere in the US presidential election in favor of Republic candidate Donald TRUMP."	■	This information was provided by ▓▓ sub-source. The sub-source has been identified as ▓▓▓▓▓▓

*Report Date
**Date Report Provided to FBI by Steele

Report Provided to Journalists, Not FBI
Report Not Provided to Corn

	Report		Information		Corroboration/Analyst Notes
					Identifying Primary Subsource and Subsource ▮▮▮
					Sensitive FBI Information ▮▮▮
					279, 280
▮	2016/132 *10/13/2016 **10/19/2016	▮	"...PUTIN's mistake had been to regard the US political system as more like Russia (corrupt) than something different and to think he understood it sufficiently well to interfere effectively"		This information was provided by Primary Subsource's sub-source. The sub-source has been identified as ▮▮▮
▮	2016/134 *10/18/2016 **10/19/2016	▮	"...reported secret meeting between [SECHIN] and Carter PAGE...in Moscow in July 2016"		This information was provided by Primary Subsource's sub-source. The sub-source was identified as ▮▮▮
					▮ Steele and open source articles report this meeting. Open source reporting originates from a September Yahoo article.[281]
					Sequestered by court order ▮▮▮
					282, 283
▮	2016/134 *10/18/2016 **10/19/2016	▮	"It took place on either 7 or 8 July, the same day or the one after Carter PAGE made a public speech to the Higher Economic School in Moscow."		This information was provided by Primary Subsource's sub-source. The sub-source was identified as ▮ Identifying Primary Subsource and Subsource ▮▮▮

*Report Date
**Date Report Provided to FBI by Steele

Report Provided to Journalists, Not FBI
Report Not Provided to Corn

PRODUCED TO SJC/SSCI

Report	Information	Corroboration/Analyst Notes
		There is a school named the Higher School of Economics located in Moscow. [284]
		Via open source articles in July, PAGE gave a commencement speech on 8 July at the New Economic School in Moscow. [285]
2016/134 *10/18/2016 **10/19/2016	"...the Rosneft President was so keen to lift personal and corporate western sanctions imposed on the company, that he offered PAGE/TRUMP's associates the brokerage of up to a 19 per cent (privatized) stake in Rosneft in return."	This information was provided by Primary Subsource's sub-source. The sub-source was identified as Primary Subsource's subsource identifying Primary Subsource and Subsource
		On 09 March 2017, Page was interviewed by FBI NY. Page stated that Glencore received the stake, which is associated to Mark Rich, an associate of the Clintons. Page claimed his was evidence of the Clinton's pay-to-play schemes. Mark Rich was a founder of the Clinton Library. [286]
		In September 2014 interview, Rosneft President Igor Sechin was quoted saying "Neither I nor my company have anything to do with the crisis in Ukraine. As such, there is no foundation for the sanctions against me and Rosneft. They represent a violation of international law." [287]
2016/134 *10/18/2016 **10/19/2016	"PAGE had expressed interest and confirmed that were TRUMP elected US president, then sanctions on Russia would be lifted."	This information was provided by Primary Subsource's sub-source. The sub-source was identified as Primary Subsource's subsource identifying Primary Subsource and Subsource
		In open source reporting, Page has discussed the negative implications US sanctions on Russia have had on his own business. He has expressed strong opinions against sanctions, citing it as an "injustice unleashed upon millions of people residing in Russia. [288,289]

*Report Date
**Date Report Provided to FBI by Steele

Report Provided to Journalists, Not FBI
Report Not Provided to Corn

Report	Information	Corroboration/Analyst Notes
2016/134 *10/18/2016 **10/19/2016	"...Rosneft President had continued to believe that TRUMP could win the US presidency right up to 17 October, when he assessed this was no longer possible."	This information was provided by Primary Subsource's sub-source. The sub-source was identified as [redacted] Primary Subsource's subsource identifying Primary Subsource and Subsource
2016/134 *10/18/2016 **10/19/2016	"SECHIN was keen to re-adapt accordingly and put feelers out to other business and political contacts in the US instead."	This information was provided by Primary Subsource's sub-source. The sub-source was identified as [redacted] Primary Subsource's subsource identifying Primary Subsource and Subsource
2016/134 *10/18/2016 **10/19/2016	"...key role in the secret TRUMP campaign/Kremlin relationship was being played by the Republican candidate's personal lawyer Michael COHEN."	This information was provided by Primary Subsource's sub-source. The sub-source was identified as [redacted] Primary Subsource's subsource identifying Primary Subsource and Sub [redacted] Cohen currently serves as Special Counsel to Donald Trump and Executive Vice President of the Trump Organization. As Executive Vice President, Cohen also serves as the co-president of Trump Entertainment. He had been the lead negotiator for the Trump Tower project in Batumi, Georgia, and also serves as the Chief Operating Officer of Affliction Entertainment. Prior to beginning work for the Trump Organization in 2007, Cohen was a partner at Phillips Nizer.[290,291,292,293] Cohen also has some experience in politics. In 1988, he volunteered for the presidential campaign of Michael Dukakis, and later served as a legislative intern for US Congressman John Joseph Moakley. Cohen ran for New York City Council as a Republican in 2003, and briefly ran for the US Senate as a Democrat in 2009. Cohen began meeting with Republican operatives in 2011 to determine the reception of a potential Trump presidential campaign.[294]

*Report Date
**Date Report Provided to FBI by Steele

Report Provided to Journalists, Not FBI
Report Not Provided to Corn

	Report		Information		Corroboration/Analyst Notes
					▮ 2016/135 and 2016/136 reference a secret meeting in Prague between Cohen and Kremlin officials in August 2016.
					▮▮▮) The CROSSFIRE HURRICANE team has been unable to verify travel by Cohen to the Czech Republic in August 2016. Other Agency Information ▮▮▮ 295
▮	2016/134 *10/18/2016 **10/19/2016	▮	"COHEN had a wife of Russia origin, whose father, Efim SHUSTERMAN, was a leading Moscow property developer."		▮▮▮ This information was provided by Primary Subsource's sub-source. The sub-source was identified as Primary Subsource's subsource Identifying Primary Subsource and Sub ▮▮▮.
					▮ Cohen's wife is Laura Cohen [nee Shusterman], PII ▮▮▮ Her father is Fima – a shortened version of Efim – Shusterman PII ▮ 296
▮	2016/134 *10/18/2016 **10/19/2016	▮	"...SHUSTERMAN has a country house (dacha) in the settlement of Barvikha, west of Moscow...village reserved for the residences of the top leadership and their close associates."		▮▮ This information was provided by Primary Subsource's sub-source. The sub-source was identified as Primary Subsource's subsource Identifying Primary Subsource and Sub ▮▮▮.
					▮ Barvikha is a "small town of villas and luxury boutiques" and "home to half a dozen or so deposed leaders and members of their families", including Askar Akayev, the former President of Kyrgyzstan. It is "home to politicians, including President Vladimir Putin, and members of Russia's business elite."[297][298]
					▮ *Barvikha Luxury Village*, located in Barvikha, is a large-scale country project of the Mercury company, featuring the following:

*Report Date
**Date Report Provided to FBI by Steele

Report Provided to Journalists, Not FBI
Report Not Provided to Corn

⬛ Report	⬛ Information	⬛ Corroboration/Analyst Notes
		<ul><li>Barvikha Hotel & Spa and Spa Dominique Chenot</li><li>Pedestrian street of boutiques, car dealers and banks</li><li>Gourmet restaurants and wine collection</li><li>Market for environmental products</li><li>A unique concert hall.</li></ul> ⬛ The area totals more than 80,000 sqm and is located in the prestigious district of Moscow region, only 8 kilometers west from Moscow Rublevo Uspenskomu.[299]
⬛ 2016/135 *10/19/16 **10/19/16	⬛ "Cohen engaged with Russians in trying to cover up a scandal of Manafort and exposure of Page and meets Kremlin officials secretly in the EU in August in pursuit of this goal."	⬛ This information was provided by ⬛Primary Subsource's sub-source. The sub-source was identified as ⬛Primary Subsource's subsource identifying Primary Subsource and Sub ⬛ ⬛ The CROSSFIRE HURRICANE team has been unable to verify travel by Cohen to the Czech Republic in August 2016. ⬛Other Agency Information ⬛[300]
⬛ 2016/135 *10/19/16 **10/19/16	⬛ "These secret contacts continue but are now farmed out to trusted agents in Kremlin-linked institutes so as to remain 'plausibly deniable' for Russian regime"	
⬛ 2016/135 *10/19/16 **10/19/16	⬛ "Sacking of Ivanov and appointments of Vaino and Kiriyenko linked to need to cover up Kremlin's Trump support operation."	⬛ This information was provided by ⬛Primary Subsource's sub-source. The sub-source was identified as ⬛Primary Subsource's subsource identifying Primary Subsource and Sub ⬛ ⬛ In August 2016, Kremlin chief of staff or Chief of Staff of the Presidential Administration Sergei Ivanov, an ally and fellow former KGB officer who had held several key posts in Putin's Russia, was replaced with Anton Vaino, a little-known deputy presidential administration chief in charge of protocol.[301]

*Report Date
**Date Report Provided to FBI by ⬛Steele

Report Provided to Journalists, Not FBI
Report Not Provided to Corn

▮ Report	▮ Information	▮ Corroboration/Analyst Notes
		▮ Sergei Ivanov was replaced by Anton Vaino on August 12, 2016. [302] ▮ Sergei Kiriyenko was appointed to the first Deputy Head of the Presidential Administration on 12 September 2016. [303] **Other Agency Information** ▮▮▮▮▮▮▮▮▮▮▮▮▮▮▮▮▮▮▮▮▮▮▮▮▮▮▮▮▮▮▮▮▮▮▮▮▮▮ [304]
▮ 2016/135 *10/19/16 **10/19/16	▮ "a Kremlin insider highlighted the importance of Republican presidential candidate Donald Trump's lawyer, Michael Cohen, in the ongoing secret liaison relationship between the New York tycoon's campaign and the Russian leadership."	▮ This information was provided by ▮Primary Subsource's▮ sub-source. The sub-source was identified as ▮Primary Subsource's subsource identifying Primary Subsource and Sub▮ ▮▮▮▮▮▮▮▮▮▮▮▮▮▮▮▮▮▮▮▮▮▮▮▮▮▮▮▮▮▮ ▮ Cohen currently serves as Special Counsel to Donald Trump and Executive Vice President of the Trump Organization. As Executive Vice President, Cohen also serves as the co-president of Trump Entertainment. He had been the lead negotiator for the Trump Tower project in Batumi, Georgia, and also serves as the Chief Operating Officer of Affliction Entertainment. Prior to beginning work for the Trump Organization in 2007, Cohen was a partner at Phillips Nizer. [305, 306, 307, 308]

*Report Date
**Date Report Provided to FBI by ▮Steele▮

Report Provided to Journalists, Not FBI
Report Not Provided to Corn

PRODUCED TO SJC/SSCI

Report	Information	Corroboration/Analyst Notes
		Cohen also has some experience in politics. In 1988, he volunteered for the presidential campaign of Michael Dukakis, and later served as a legislative intern for US Congressman John Joseph Moakley. Cohen ran for New York City Council as a Republican in 2003, and briefly ran for the US Senate as a Democrat in 2009. Cohen began meeting with Republican operatives in 2011 to determine the reception of a potential Trump presidential campaign.[309]
2016/135 *10/19/16 **10/19/16	"Cohen's role had grown following the departure of Paul Manafort as Trump's campaign manager in August of 2016"	Paul Manafort resigned from the Trump campaign on 19 August 2016.[310]
2016/135 *10/19/16 **10/19/16	"Prior to that Manafort had led for the Trump side"	Paul Manafort was chief strategist and campaign chairman for the Donald Trump presidential campaign from 8 May to 19 August 2016.[311] On May 19, 2016 Manafort was named campaign chairman and chief strategist for the Donald Trump presidential campaign.[312] Manafort originally joined the Trump campaign on March 28, 2016 to lead the delegate effort for the Republican National Convention.[313] Manafort moved into a condo in Trump Towers in 2006, but it does not appear that Manafort had prior business dealings with Trump or his enterprises.[314]
2016/135 *10/19/16 **10/19/16	"Cohen now was heavily engaged in the cover up and damage limitation operation in the attempt to prevent the full details of Trump's relationship with Russia being exposed"	This information was provided by Primary Subsource's sub-source. The sub-source was identified as Primary Subsource's subsource identifying Primary Subsource and Sub
2016/135 *10/19/16 **10/19/16	"In pursuit of this aim, Cohen had met secretly with several Russian Presidential Administration Legal Department officials in the EU country in August 2016"	This information was provided by Primary Subsource's sub-source. The sub-source was identified as Primary Subsource's subsource identifying Primary Subsource and Sub

*Report Date
**Date Report Provided to FBI by Steele

Report Provided to Journalists, Not FBI
Report Not Provided to Corn

	Report		Information		Corroboration/Analyst Notes
					The CROSSFIRE HURRICANE team has been unable to verify travel by Cohen to the Czech Republic in August 2016. Other Agency Information [315]
	2016/135 *10/19/16 **10/19/16		"The immediate issues had been to contain further scandals involving Mannafort's commercial and political role in Russia/Ukraine and to limit the damage arising from exposure of former Trump foreign policy advisor, Carter Page's secret meetings with Russian leadership figures in Moscow the previous month"		On 15 August 2016 several articles were published detailing Manafort's prior dealings with the Pro-Russia Party of Regions in Ukraine, and his potential links to illegal payments. [316]
					In 2005 Ukrainian Oligarch Rinat Akhmetov hired Manafort to improve his public image and the image of his companies in Ukraine. Akhmetov introduced Manafort to future Ukrainian Prime Minister Viktor Yanukovych, and soon after Manafort began consulting for the Party of Regions (POR), the pro-Russian political party in Ukraine. During this period Manafort received payments of 10 million and 17 million dollars from Vega Holdings a company whose ownership could not be determined. [317, 318]
					During the 2006 Ukrainian parliamentary election, Manafort consulted for the POR. He received 2.5 million dollars from Antes Management Corp. OST West, a company purportedly owned by the POR. [319]
					In 2007 Manafort entered into a business partnership with Russian Oligarch Oleg Deripaska. Manafort and two American business partners, Richard Davis and Richard Gates, created a private equity fund in the Cayman Islands called Pericles Emerging Market Investors. Deripaska invested in this fund through his own Cyprus incorporated firm, B-Invest. Deripaska agreed to pay a two percent fee for Manafort's fund management. The fund purchased stake in a Ukrainian media company in Odessa, Black Sea Cable. As of 2014 Deripaska was in an active law suit with Manafort, Gates, and Davis, claiming that they had taken 19 million dollars from the fund and 7.3 million in fees, with no financial return for Deripaska. [320, 321]

*Report Date
**Date Report Provided to FBI by Steele

Report Provided to Journalists, Not FBI
Report Not Provided to Corn

■ Report	■ Information	■ Corroboration/Analyst Notes
		■ Beginning in 2008, Manafort began business negotiations with Ukrainian national Dmitry Firtash. Manafort and his American business partners sought to purchase the Drake Hotel, tear it down, and build a luxury apartment building. Firtash created an investment fund for the venture, but the deal never materialized. In December of 2011, former Ukrainian Prime Minister Yulia Tymoshenko filed a lawsuit in New York, claiming that Firtash was investing ill-gotten profits from Ukrainian energy deals. The case was eventually dismissed for lack of evidence, but the lawsuit did mention the 2008 venture with Manafort.[322] [323] ■ From 2007-2014 it appears that Manafort continued to consult for Viktor Yanukovych and the POR. After Yanukovych fled to Russia in February of 2014, it was reported that Serhiy Lyovochkin, Yanukovych's former chief of staff, put Manafort on retainer for the POR (now called the Opposition Block or Oppo Block).[324] [325] [326] [327]
■ 2016/135 *10/19/16 **10/19/16	■ "Things had become even 'hotter' since August on the Trump-Russia track."	■ There were articles about Paul Manafort's connections to Ukraine and Russia on 4 August, 15 August, 16 August, and 17 August 2016.[328] [329] [330] [331] ■ As of August 2016 Manafort is the active subject of a money laundering and tax evasion criminal case out of Washington Field Office (WFO).[332] ■ In July of 2016 it was reported that a document was recovered during the investigation of Ukrainian justice official indicating that Manafort had hired the law firm Skadden, Arps, Meaghe & Flom to draft a report defending the prosecution and incarceration of former Ukrainian Prime Minster Yulia Tymoshenko.[333] [334] ■ In August 2016, the Ukrainian National Anti-Corruption Bureau discovered a ledger purportedly belonging to the POR. During investigation of this ledger they claimed that Manafort's name is

*Report Date
**Date Report Provided to FBI by Steele

Report Provided to Journalists, Not FBI
Report Not Provided to Corn

PRODUCED TO SSCI

▮ Report	▮ Information	▮ Corroboration/Analyst Notes
		mentioned twenty two times between the years 2007-2012, with amounts totaling 12.7 million dollars.[335, 336, 337] ▮ On August 17 2016, the Associated Press reported that in 2012 Manafort help route 2.2 million dollars to two separate lobbying firms in Washington DC. The report states that Manafort did this on behalf of the Ukrainian POR, and sought to obscure the source of the funds. Allegedly, Manafort and his deputy Richard Gates used a pro-Yanukovych non-profit, the European Centre for a Modern Ukraine, to hire the firms to lobby on behalf of the POR and the prime minister at the time Viktor Yanukovych.[338, 339]
▮ 2016/135 *10/19/16 **10/19/16	▮ "this had meant that direct contact between the Trump team and Russia had been farmed out by the Kremlin to trusted agents of influence working in pro-government policy institutes like that of Law and Comparative Jurisprudence. Cohen however continued to lead for the Trump team."	▮ This information was provided by Primary Subsource's sub-source. The sub-source was identified as Primary Subsource's subsource identifying Primary Subsource and Subs ▮▮▮▮▮▮ ▮ There is an Institute of Legislation and Comparative Jurisprudence in Russia. It appears to be closely tied to the Russian Government.[340] ▮ This is most likely the Institute of Legislation and Comparative Law (sometimes called the Institute of Legislation and Comparative Law under the RF Government) in Moscow. The website is noted as www.izak.ru. Sources and Methods ▮▮▮▮▮▮ ▮ This entity goes by multiple names, translated from Russian into English. It can be called the RF State-Law Administration [or Department], the RF Government-Legal Department, the Legal

*Report Date
**Date Report Provided to FBI by Steele

Report Provided to Journalists, Not FBI
Report Not Provided to Corn

	Report		Information		Corroboration/Analyst Notes
					Directorate, or the Legal Administration. According to open source information dated mid-August 2016, the chief of the Kremlin's legal department is Larisa Brycheva, who has served in that capacity for many years.
	2016/135 *10/19/16 **10/19/16		"Referring back to the (surprise) sacking of Sergei Ivanov as head of PA in August 2016, his replacement by Anton Vaino and the appointment of former Russian premier Sergei Kiriyenko to another senior position in the PA, the Kremlin insider repeated that this had been directly connected to the Trump support operation and the need to cover up now that it was being exposed by the USG and in the western media."		This information was provided by ▮Primary Subsource's sub-source. The sub-source was identified as ▮▮▮ ▮) In August 2016, Kremlin chief of staff or Chief of Staff of the Presidential Administration Sergei Ivanov, an ally and fellow former KGB officer who had held several key posts in Putin's Russia, was replaced with Anton Vaino, a little-known deputy presidential administration chief in charge of protocol.[341] Sergei Ivanov was replaced by Anton Vaino on August 12, 2016.[342] Sergei Kiriyenko was appointed to the first Deputy Head of the Presidential Administration on 12 September 2016.[343] **Other Agency Information**

*Report Date
**Date Report Provided to FBI by Steele

Report Provided to Journalists, Not FBI
Report Not Provided to Corn

SENATE-FISA2020-001646

Report	Information	Corroboration/Analyst Notes
		Other Agency Information ▮▮▮▮▮▮▮▮ 344
▮ 2016/136 *10/20/16 **10/21/16	▮ "Kremlin insider reports Trump lawyer Cohen's secret meeting/s with Kremlin officials in August 2016 was/were held in Prague"	▮ This information was provided by Primary Subsource's sub-source. The sub-source was identified as Primary Subsource's subsource identifying Primary Subsource and Sub ▮▮▮▮▮▮▮▮▮▮▮▮▮▮▮▮▮▮▮▮ ▮ The CROSSFIRE HURRICANE team has been unable to verify travel by Cohen to the Czech Republic in August 2016. Other Agency Information ▮▮▮▮▮▮▮▮▮▮▮▮▮▮▮▮▮▮ 5
▮ 2016/136 *10/20/16 **10/21/16	▮ "Russian parastatal organization Rossotrudnichestvo used as cover for this liaison and premises in Czech capital may have been used for the meeting"	▮ This information was provided by Primary Subsource's sub-source. The sub-source was identified as Primary Subsource's subsource identifying Primary Subsource and Sub ▮▮▮▮▮▮▮▮▮▮▮▮▮▮▮▮▮▮▮▮ ▮ According to open source information (cze.rs.gov.ru) dated 2 December 2013, Leonid Anatolyevich Gamza was noted as the Rossotrudnichestvo representative in the Czech Republic. Other Agency Information ▮▮▮▮▮▮▮▮▮▮▮▮▮▮▮▮▮▮ 346
▮ 2016/136 *10/20/16 **10/21/16	▮ "speaking to a compatriot and friend on Oct 19 2016, a Kremlin insider provided further details of reported clandestine meeting/s between Republican presidential candidate Donald Trump's lawyer Michael Cohen and Kremlin representatives in August 2016"	▮ This information was provided by Primary Subsource's sub-source. The sub-source was identified as Primary Subsource's subsource identifying Primary Subsource and Sub ▮▮▮▮▮▮▮▮▮▮▮▮▮▮▮▮▮▮▮▮

*Report Date
**Date Report Provided to FBI by Steele

Report Provided to Journalists, Not FBI
Report Not Provided to Corn

PRODUCED TO SJO/SSCI

	Report		Information	Corroboration/Analyst Notes
				The CROSSFIRE HURRICANE team has been unable to verify travel by Cohen to the Czech Republic in August 2016. Other Agency Information 347
	2016/136 *10/20/16 **10/21/16		"the Kremlin insider clearly indicated to his/her friend that the reported contact/s took place in Prague, Czech Republic"	This information was provided by Primary Subsource's sub-source. The sub-source was identified as Primary Subsource's subsource; identifying Primary Subsource and Sub ev.
				The CROSSFIRE HURRICANE team has been unable to verify travel by Cohen to the Czech Republic in August 2016. Other Agency Information 348
	2016/136 *10/20/16 **10/21/16		"the Kremlin insider highlighted the importance of the Russian parastatal organization, Rossotrudnichestvo, in this contact between Trump campaign representative/s and Kremlin officials."	This information was provided by Primary Subsource's sub-source. The sub-source was identified as Primary Subsource's subsource; identifying Primary Subsource and Sub
				According to open source information (cze.rs.gov.ru) dated 2 December 2013, Leonid Anatolyevich Gamza was noted as the Rossotrudnichestvo representative in the Czech Republic. Other Agency Information 349
	2016/136 *10/20/16 **10/21/16		"Rossotrudnichestvo was being used as cover for this relationship and its office in Prague may well have been used to host the Cohen/Russian Presidential Administration meeting/s."	This information was provided by Primary Subsource's sub-source. The sub-source was identified as Primary Subsource's subsource; identifying Primary Subsource and Sub

*Report Date
**Date Report Provided to FBI by Steele

Report Provided to Journalists, Not FBI
Report Not Provided to Corn

■ Report	■ Information	Corroboration/Analyst Notes
		■ According to open source information (cze.rs.gov.ru) dated 2 December 2013, Leonid Anatolyevich Gamza was noted as the Rossotrudnichestvo representative in the Czech Republic. ▮Other Agency Information▮ ██████████ 350 ██████) The CROSSFIRE HURRICANE team has been unable to verify travel by Cohen to the Czech Republic in August 2016. ▮Other Agency Information▮ ██████ 351
■ 2016/136 *10/20/16 **10/21/16	■ "It was considered a 'plausibly deniable' vehicle for this, whilst remaining entirely under Kremlin control."	
■ 2016/136 *10/20/16 **10/21/16	■ "The Kremlin insider went on to identify leading pro-Putin Duma figure, Konstantin Kosachev (Head of Foreign Relations Committee) as an important figure in the Trump campaign-Kremlin liaison operation."	██ This information was provided by ▮Primary Subsource's▮ sub-source. The sub-source was identified as ▮Primary Subsource's subsource identifying Primary Subsource and Sub▮ ████████ ██ Kosachev was named to the Russian Duma in late December 2014. Upon becoming a Russian senator, he replaced Mikhail Margelov as the chairman of the Foreign Affairs Committee of Russia's Federation Council. 352 ██ In 2012 Kosachev was named head of Rossotrudnichestvo. 353 ███████ The alleged use of Rossotrudnichestvo in Prague and the source's references to Konstantin Kosachev's involvement makes sense given that Kosachev served as the chief of Rossotrudnichestvo between March 2012 and March 2015 – at which time he was replaced by Lyubov Glebova. Rossotrudnichevo's representative in Prague, Leonid Gamza, served in Prague under Kosachev's tenure in

*Report Date
**Date Report Provided to FBI by ▮Steele▮

Report Provided to Journalists, Not FBI
Report Not Provided to Corn

SENATE-FISA2020-001649

	Report		Information		Corroboration/Analyst Notes
					Rossotrudnichestvo, so it is very likely that the two of them know one another. Other Agency Information
					Other Agency Information [354]
	2016/136 *10/20/16 **10/21/16		"Kosachev, also 'plausibly deniable' being part of the Russian legislature rather than executive, had facilitated the contact in Prague and by implication, may have attended the meeting/s with Cohen there in August"		This information was provided by Primary Subsource's sub-source. The sub-source was identified as Primary Subsource's subsource identifying Primary Subsource and Sub
					Kosachev was named to the Russian Duma in late December 2014. Upon becoming a Russian senator, he replaced Mikhail Margelov as the chairman of the Foreign Affairs Committee of Russia's Federation Council. [355]
					In 2012 Kosachev was named head of Rossotrudnichestvo. [356]
					At this time the CROSSFIRE HURRICANE team is unable to corroborate travel for Kosachev.
	2016/136 *10/20/16 **10/21/16		"According to the Kremlin advisor, these meeting/s were originally scheduled for Cohen in Moscow but shifted to what was considered an operationally 'soft' EU country when it was judged too compromising for him to travel to the Russian capital"		This information was provided by Primary Subsource's sub-source. The sub-source was identified as Primary Subsource's subsource identifying Primary Subsource and Sub
					The CROSSFIRE HURRICANE team has been unable to verify travel by Cohen to the Czech Republic in August 2016. Other Agency Information

*Report Date
**Date Report Provided to FBI by Steele

Report Provided to Journalists, Not FBI
Report Not Provided to Corn

	Report		Information		Corroboration/Analyst Notes
					Sources and Methods [357]
	2016/137 *10/14/16 **10/24/16		"Former Trump foreign policy adviser Page's secret Kremlin contact, Divyekin, moved from PA to a senior Duma position following his exposure in Western media"		This information was provided by [Primary Subsource's] sub-source. The sub-source was identified as [redacted] On September 23rd, 2016 Yahoo News published an article claiming Carter Page was under investigation by the FBI and US Intelligence due to his ties with Russia. This article mentioned Page's alleged meeting with Divyekin.[358] [Analyst Note: There is no open source reporting mentioning Divyekin or his move to the Duma. However it is noted that Diveykin once worked for Volodin's secretariat, it is possible that Diveykin's move to the Duma was to follow his former boss.
	2016/137 *10/14/16 **10/24/16		"New position gives Divyekin diplomatic immunity if he travels abroad, making it harder for the USG to detain or question him. Move assessed by Kremlin insider as unorthodox, unsignalled and therefore as part of Kremlin Trump support operation cover-up."		This information was provided by [Primary Subsource's] sub-source. The sub-source was identified as [redacted] Unable to corroborate, there appears to be no press or announcements listing an administrative move for Divyekin.
	2016/137 *10/14/16 **10/24/16		"In mid October 2016, a mini-reshuffle of key staff took place in the Kremlin."		This information was provided by [Primary Subsource's] sub-source. The sub-source was identified as [redacted] On 10 October 2016, Putin shuffled positions in leadership, including the Duma. There is no mention of Divyekin, but Vyachaslav Volodin and Sergei Kiriyenko's names are mentioned.[359] 23 March 2015 – An article in Gazeta.ru detailed the departure of Oleg Morozov, the head of the Russian Presidential Administration's Domestic Policy Administration. Morozov, who had served in the

*Report Date
**Date Report Provided to FBI by Steele

Report Provided to Journalists, Not FBI
Report Not Provided to Corn

▮ Report	▮ Information	▮ Corroboration/Analyst Notes
		position since May 2012, was replaced by Tatyana Voronova. In turn, the article named Igor Diveykin, "current leader of [first deputy head of the Presidential Staff Vyacheslav] Volodin's secretariat."[360] ▮ Vyachaslav Volodin was voted to be the speaker of the Duma, replacing Sergei Naryshkin, who was named as the new head of the SVR.[361] ▮ There is no open source reporting mentioning Divyekin or his move to the Duma. However it is noted that Diveykin once worked for Volodin's secretariat, it is possible that Divyekin's move to the Duma was to follow his former boss.
▮ 2016/137 *10/14/16 **10/24/16	▮ "As part of this reshuffle, the deputy Head of the Presidential Administration Internal Affairs department, Igor Divyekin, was moved from this position to a new one as Charge D'Affaires at the State Duma."	▮ This information was provided by Primary Subsource's sub-source. The sub-source was identified as ▮▮▮▮▮ Unable to corroborate, there appears to be no press or announcements listing an administrative move for Divyekin.
▮ 2016/137 *10/14/16 **10/24/16	▮ "This move followed Divyekin, a previously low key but senior Russian official, being exposed in the Western media e.g. the Yahoo News story of Sept. 23 2016 as a secret interlocutor of Carter Page."	▮ On 23 September 2016, Yahoo News published an article claiming Carter Page was under investigation by the FBI and US Intelligence due to his ties with Russia. This article mentioned Page's alleged meeting with Divyekin.[362]
▮ 2016/137 *10/14/16 **10/24/16	▮ "Commenting on this move to a trusted friend and compatriot after the event in late October 2016, a Kremlin insider highlighted that Divyekin's move was highly unusual. It did not form part of a wider rotation of staff; had not been prompted by a promotion or gazette; and Divyekin was not obviously qualified for the job."	▮ This information was provided by Primary Subsource's sub-source. The sub-source was identified as ▮▮▮▮▮
▮ 2016/137 *10/14/16 **10/24/16	▮ "The new Duma position however gave him diplomatic immunity, at least in the Russian government's eyes, making it more difficult for the USG or other foreign governments to detain or question Divyekin were he to travel abroad"	▮ This information was provided by Primary Subsource's sub-source. The sub-source was identified as ▮▮▮▮▮

*Report Date
**Date Report Provided to FBI by Steele

Report Provided to Journalists, Not FBI
Report Not Provided to Corn

	Report		Information		Corroboration/Analyst Notes
					Unable to corroborate if Divyekin received a new position.
					The Charge D' Affaires position is granted diplomatic immunity.[363]
	2016/137 *10/14/16 **10/24/16		"The Kremlin insider compared the Divyekin move to the maneuvering of chief Aleksandr Litvinenko murder suspect, Andrei Lugovoy into the Duma as a deputy after he had been exposed as a conspirator by the Western media in 2007. Logovoy's position also gave him diplomatic immunity."		Andrei Lugovoy was suspected of participating in the murder of Aleksandr Litvinenko, and after his potential role was made public, he was given a position in the Russian Duma.[364]
	2016/139 *10/27/16 **10/28/16		"...TRUMP campaign Russian émigré figure, Serge MILLIAN..."		On 29 March 2017, *The Washington Post* published an article describing Millian's comments that he was in touch with a campaign foreign policy advisor, George Papadopoulos, during the campaign and presidential transition. There is mention that Millian and Papadopoulos are friends on Facebook. Open source reporting has established a working relationship between MILLIAN and TRUMP as early as 2007. [365, 366, 367, 368, 369, 370]
	2016/139 *10/27/16 **10/28/16		"The propaganda campaign, largely funded by Alpha Group business oligarch, Mikhail FRIDMAN, at President PUTIN's request, so as to remain "plausibly deniable", however had run into trouble.		Open source reporting on Alfa Bank, owned by Alfa Group, identifies Mikhail Fridman as one of its key executives. Sensitive FBI Information [371]
	2016/139 *10/27/16 **10/28/16		"...MILLIAN, had been forced to lie low abroad following his exposure in the western media. [MILLIAN] was currently in South Korea and...was being paid, by implication by the Russian regime, not to return to the US or talk to western journalists."		Other Agency Information Other Agency Information

*Report Date
**Date Report Provided to FBI by Steele

Report Provided to Journalists, Not FBI
Report Not Provided to Corn

SENATE-FISA2020-001653

▮ Report	▮ Information	Corroboration/Analyst Notes
		Other Agency Information ███████████████ ████████████████████
		Other Agency Information ██████████████████
		Other Agency Information ████████████████████
		▮ Other Agency Information ██████████████████
		▮ Millian has reached out U.S. journalists via the social media platform, Twitter. On 1 April 2017, Millian wrote a message directly to Chuck Ross, also cc'ing the twitter handle for The Daily Caller, Fox News, and Sean Hannity. He also included both Twitter accounts associated with POTUS. On 31 March 2017 Millian wrote a message

*Report Date
**Date Report Provided to FBI by ▮Steele▮

Report Provided to Journalists, Not FBI
Report Not Provided to Corn

Report	Information	Corroboration/Analyst Notes
		penned for journalists at the Washington Post. His first comment regarding news reporting came on Twitter on 26 January 2017.
		An article published on 31 March 2017 by the online magazine *Brightest Young Things* appears to be Millian's only recent U.S. contact to publish his statements.[377]
■ 2016/139 *10/27/16 **10/28/16	■ "...MILLIAN had played a specific role for the Kremlin on shaping TRUMP's protectionist policy stance (especially relating to TPP and TIPP which the Russian leadership strongly opposed)."	■ Millian's travel to Asia in the past year includes the following. Any travel affiliated with a TPP member-country has been bolded. Other Agency Information ■

*Report Date
**Date Report Provided to FBI by ■Steele■

Report Provided to Journalists, Not FBI
Report Not Provided to Corn

■ Report	■ Information	■ Corroboration/Analyst Notes
		■ The Trans-Pacific Partnership (TPP) includes the United States, Australia, Brunei, Canada, Chile, Japan, Malaysia, Mexico, New Zealand, Peru, Singapore, and Vietnam. The Transatlantic Trade and Investment Partnership (TTIP) is between the EU and the United States. [382]
■ 2016/139 *10/27/16 **10/28/16	■ "...US national employed by the media organization Sputnik had quoted a tweet which he thought had been put out by Wikileaks. In fact this had been premature as "it (the tweet) wasn't supposed to be released that early". As a result of this embarrassing mistake, the Sputnik employee had been sacked immediately and the propaganda programme (temporarily) suspended."	Sensitive FBI Information ████████████ [383, 384]
■ 2016/139 *10/27/16 **10/28/16	■ "...all leading Russian journalists knew that a number among them were being given privileged prior access by the Kremlin to Wikileaks material on CLINTON and leading Democratic campaign figures before it appeared on the Internet....they were under "huge pressure" not to publish anything which questioned the position of or was critical of TRUMP or favourable to Hillary CLINTON."	
■ 2016/166 *12/13/2016	■ 1. We reported previously (2016/135 and /136) pm secret meeting/s held in Prague, Czech Republic in August 2016 between then Republican presidential candidate Donald TRUMP's representative, Michael COHEN and his interlocutors from the Kremlin under cover of Russian 'NGO' Rossotrudnichestvo.	████ This information was provided by Primary Subsource's sub-source. The sub-source was identified as Primary Subsource's subsource identifying Primary Subsource and Sub ██████████
■ 2016/166 *12/13/2016	■ 2. [REDACTED] provided further details of these meeting/s and associated anti-CLINTON/ Democratic Party operations. COHEN had been accompanied to Prague by 3 colleagues and the timing of the visit was either in the last week of August or first week of September. One of their main Russian interlocutors was Oleg SOLODUKHIN operating un Rossotrudnichestvo cover. According to [REDACTED], the agenda comprised questions on how deniable cash payments	████ This information was provided by Primary Subsource's sub-source. The sub-source was identified as Primary Subsource's subsource identifying Primary Subsource and Sub ██████████

*Report Date
**Date Report Provided to FBI by Steele

Report Provided to Journalists, Not FBI
Report Not Provided to Corn

	Report		Information		Corroboration/Analyst Notes
			were to be made to hackers who worked in Europe under Kremlin direction against the CLINTON campaign and various contingences for covering up the operations and Moscow's secret liaison with the TRUMP team more generally.		
▮	2016/166 *12/13/2016	▮	3. [REDACTED] reported that over the period March-September 2016 a company called XBT/Webzilla and its affiliates had been using botnets and porn traffic to transmit viruses, plant bugs, steal data and conduct altering operations against the Democratic Party leadership. Entities linked to one Aleksei GUBAREV were involved and he and another hacking expert, both recruited under duress by the FSB, Seva KAPSUGOVICH were significant players in this operation. In Prague, COHEN agreed contingency plans for various scenarios to protect the operation, but in particular what was to be done in the event that Hilary CLINTON won the presidency. It was important in this event that all cash payments owed were made quickly and discreetly and that cyber and other operators were stood down/ able to go effectively to ground to cover their traces.	▮	▮ This information was provided by ▮Primary Subsource's sub-source. The sub-source was identified as ▮Primary Subsource's subsource identifying Primary Subsource and Sub ▮▮▮▮▮ ▮ XBT Holding was established in 2005 in Limassol, Cyprus by Aleksej [Alexei] Gubarev. XBT is a computer networking company that provides business IT services, including global server hosting, shared hosting, cloud-based storage, virtual private networks (VPNs), network and web development, IP address transit, content delivery, and application development. For the consumer, XBT provides basic domain registration and shared hosting. XBT is described as a corporation centered on software development, advertising, and E-commerce. [385, 386, 387] ▮) According the XBT's official website the main office is located in Luxembourg. XBT also has offices in the United States, Netherlands, Bulgaria, Ukraine, India, and Singapore. XBT also maintains physical data centers in the United States (Dallas), Asia, and Europe with approximately 75,000 servers in operation. Gubarev claims the United States' operation accounts for 40% of business handled over servers and 27% of total revenue for XBT, with estimated revenues of $50 to $200 million. [388, 389, 390]
▮	2016/166 *12/13/2016	▮	4. In terms of practical measures to be taken, it was agreed by the two sides in Prague to stand down various "Romanian hackers" (presumably based in their homeland or neighbouring Eastern Europe) and that other operatives should head for a	▮	▮ This information was provided by ▮ sub-source. The sub-source was identified as ▮Primary Subsource's subsource identifying Primary Subsource and Sub ▮▮▮

*Report Date
**Date Report Provided to FBI by ▮Steele

Report Provided to Journalists, Not FBI
Report Not Provided to Corn

	Report		Information		Corroboration/Analyst Notes
			bolt-hole in Plovidv, Bulgaria where they should "lay low". On payments, IVANOV's associate said that the operatives involved had been paid by both TRUMP's team and the Kremlin, though their orders and ultimate loyalty lay with IVANOV, as Head of the PA, and thus ultimately responsible for the operation, and his designated successor/s after he was dismissed by president PUTIN in connection with the anti-CLINTON operation in mid-August.		Identifying Primary Subsource and Subsource

---

[1] ████ Michael Crowely; Politico; "When Donald Trump Brought Miss Universe to Moscow"; 15 May 2016; http://www.politico.com/story/2016/05/donald-trump-russia-moscow-miss-universe-223173

[2] ████ Tom Hamburger, Rosalind S. Helderman, and Michael Birnbaum; Washington Post; "Inside Trump's Financial ties to Russia and his unusual flattery of Vladimir Putin"; 17 June 2016; https://www.washingtonpost.com/politics/inside-trumps-financial-ties-to-russia-and-his-unusual-flattery-of-vladimir-putin/2016/06/17

[3] ████ Online newspaper article; The Washington Post; "Inside Trump's financial ties to Russia and his unusual flattery of Vladimir Putin"; 17 June 2016; https://www.washingtonpost.com/politics/inside-trumps-financial-ties-to-russia-and-his-unusual-flattery-of-vladimir-putin/2016/06/17/dbdcaac8-31a6-11e6-8ff7-7b6c1998b7a0_story.html.

[4] ████ Michael Crowely; Politico; "When Donald Trump Brought Miss Universe to Moscow"; 15 May 2016; http://www.politico.com/story/2016/05/donald-trump-russia-moscow-miss-universe-223173

[5] ████ Tom Hamburger, Rosalind S. Helderman, and Michael Birnbaum; Washington Post; "Inside Trump's Financial ties to Russia and his unusual flattery of Vladimir Putin"; 17 June 2016; https://www.washingtonpost.com/politics/inside-trumps-financial-ties-to-russia-and-his-unusual-flattery-of-vladimir-putin/2016/06/17

[6] ████ Online newspaper article; The Washington Post; "Inside Trump's financial ties to Russia and his unusual flattery of Vladimir Putin"; 17 June 2016; https://www.washingtonpost.com/politics/inside-trumps-financial-ties-to-russia-and-his-unusual-flattery-of-vladimir-putin/2016/06/17/dbdcaac8-31a6-11e6-8ff7-7b6c1998b7a0_story.html.

[7] ████████████

[8] Steele Reporting- 18 October 2016

[9] ████████ Australia: Hotline to Moscow bank revealed as FBI probes Kremlin's five-year Trump ████████ 01 November 2016;

[10] ████████████████████████████

*Report Date
**Date Report Provided to FBI by Steele

Report Provided to Journalists, Not FBI
Report Not Provided to Corn

[11] ███

[12] ███

[13] ███

[14] ██ Web site. Department of State Office of the Historian. "Hillary Rodham Clinton"; https://history.state.gov/departmenthistory/travels/secreatry/clinton-hillary-rodham.

[15] ██ Web site. Department of State Office of the Historian. "William J. Clinton"; https://history.state.gov/departmenthistory/travels/president/clinton-william-j.

[16] ██ Web site; President of Russia; "Presidential Address to the Federal Assembly"; 04 December 2014; en.kremlin.ru/events/president/news/47173

[17] ██ Web site; President of Russia; "Message from the President of Russia to the leaders of several European countries"; 10 April 2014; en.kremlin.ru/events/president/news/20751

[18] ██ Web site; President of Russia; "Vladimir Putin's interview with Radio Europe 1 and TF1 TV channel"; 04 June 2014; en.kremlin.ru/events/president/news/45832

[19] ██ Michael Crowely; Politico; "When Donald Trump Brought Miss Universe to Moscow"; 15 May 2016; http://www.politico.com/story/2016/05/donald-trump-russia-moscow-miss-universe-223173

[20] ██ Tom Hamburger, Rosalind S. Helderman, and Michael Birnbaum; Washington Post; "Inside Trump's Financial ties to Russia and his unusual flattery of Vladimir Putin"; 17 June 2016; https://www.washingtonpost.com/politics/inside-trumps-financial-ties-to-russia-and-his-unusual-flattery-of-vladimir-putin/2016/06/17

[21] ██ Online newspaper article; The Washington Post; "Inside Trump's financial ties to Russia and his unusual flattery of Vladimir Putin"; 17 June 2016; https://www.washingtonpost.com/politics/inside-trumps-financial-ties-to-russia-and-his-unusual-flattery-of-vladimir-putin/2016/06/17/dbdcaac8-31a6-11e6-8ff7-7b6c1998b7a0_story.html.

[22] ██ Michael Crowely; Politico; "When Donald Trump Brought Miss Universe to Moscow"; 15 May 2016; http://www.politico.com/story/2016/05/donald-trump-russia-moscow-miss-universe-223173

[23] ██ Tom Hamburger, Rosalind S. Helderman, and Michael Birnbaum; Washington Post; "Inside Trump's Financial ties to Russia and his unusual flattery of Vladimir Putin"; 17 June 2016; https://www.washingtonpost.com/politics/inside-trumps-financial-ties-to-russia-and-his-unusual-flattery-of-vladimir-putin/2016/06/17

[24] ██ Online newspaper article; The Washington Post; "Inside Trump's financial ties to Russia and his unusual flattery of Vladimir Putin"; 17 June 2016; https://www.washingtonpost.com/politics/inside-trumps-financial-ties-to-russia-and-his-unusual-flattery-of-vladimir-putin/2016/06/17/dbdcaac8-31a6-11e6-8ff7-7b6c1998b7a0_story.html.

[25] ██

[26] ██ http://www.ritzcarlton.com/en/hotels/europe/moscow/rooms-suites

*R███ort Date
**Date Report Provided to FBI by ██Steele██

Report Provided to Journalists, Not FBI
Report Not Provided to Corn

PRODUCED TO SJC/SSCI

27 http://ritzcarlton.com/en/hotels/europe/moscow/hotel-overview/press-releases/renovated-presidential-suite

28 Pravda; ""Barack Obama to stay at 13,000-dollar luxury suite at Moscow's Ritz-Carlton Hotel"; 3 July 2009.

29

30

31 Online news article. Financial Times. "Carte blanche for FSB's Directorate K"; https://www.ft.com/content/94390c4c-de23-11e0-9fb7-00144feabdc0; 13 September 2011.

32 Web site. Department of State Office of the Historian. "Hillary Rodham Clinton"; https://history.state.gov/departmenthistory/travels/secreatry/clinton-hillary-rodham.

33 Web site. Department of State Office of the Historian. "William J. Clinton"; https://history.state.gov/departmenthistory/travels/president/clinton-william-j.

34

35

36

37

38

39

40

41

42

43

44 FBI; FD-302; "Interview of Carter Page"; ; 16 March 2017; 16 March 2017;

45

46

47

48

49

*R ded to Journalists, Not FBI
Report Not Provided to Corn

**Date Report Provided to FBI by Steele

50 ██

51 ██

52 ██ www.nes.ru/en/people/catalog/m/vmakarov.

53 ██ Web site; ABCNews.com; "Trump Foreign Policy Adviser Calls for 'Mutual Respect' in Moscow Lecture"; 7 July, 2016; http://abcnews.go.com/International/trump-foreign-policy-adviser-calls-mutual-respect-moscow/story?id=40417854; accessed 8 August 2016; ABC News is a television and online news source.

54 ██ Web site; New Times; "Advisor Trump Page Carter 'I am in Moscow as a Private Citizen'" 07 July 2016. http://www.newtimes.ru/stati/novosti/d04847e76bfa3c46d83127f153c72ba8-sovetnuk-trampa-Karter-peidj-ya-v-moskve-kak-chastnii-grajdanun.html; accessed 10 November 2016; The New Times is an online Russian news source.

55 ████████ FBI; FD-302; "Interview of Carter Page"; ████████ 16 March 2017; 16 March 2017;

56 ████████ FBI; FD-302; "Interview of Carter Page"; ████████ 16 March 2017; 16 March 2017;

57 ███

58 █ FBI; Electronic Communication; ██

59 ██

60 ███

61 http://www.gazeta.ru/politics/2015/03/23_a_6611137.shtml

62 Michael Isikov; Yahoo News; "Us Intel officials probe ties between Trump adviser and Kremlin"; 23 September 2016.

63 ██

64 ██

65 ██

66 Michael Isikov; Yahoo News; "Us Intel officials probe ties between Trump adviser and Kremlin"; 23 September 2016.

67 ██ Web site; Spiegel Online; "Russia Didn't Initiate the Ukraine Crisis"" 02 September 2014; http://www.spiegel.de/international/business/rosneft-head-igor-sechin-speaks-about-sanctions-and-ukraine-a-989267.html; accessed 21 November 2016; Spiegel Online is a German online media source.

68 ████████ FBI; FD-302; "Interview of Carter Page"; ████████ 16 March 2017; 16 March 2017; ████

69 Ibid.

70 ██

71 ███

72 ████████ FBI; FD-302; "Interview of Carter Page"; ████████ 16 March 2017; 16 March 2017; ████

73 Web site; Vox.com; "Forget Conspiracy Theories. This is why Trump's Russian Connection is Actually a Problem" 1 November, 2016; http://www.vox.com/world/2016/11/1/13487322/donald-trump-russia-agent-hack; accessed 10 November 2016; Vox is an online news source.

*Report Date

**Date Report Provided to FBI by Steele

Report Provided to Journalists, Not FBI
Report Not Provided to Corn

SENATE-FISA2020-001661

[74] ▓ Web site; TheGuardian.com; "US Officially Accuses Russia of Hacking DNC and Interfering with Election" 07 October, 2016; http://www.theguardian.com/technology/2016/Oct/07/Us-Russia-dnc-hack-interfering-presidential-election; accessed 10 November 2016; The Guardian is an online and print news source.

[75] ▓ FBI; EC; ▓▓

[76] ▓ The Washington Times; "Roger Stone, Trump confidant, acknowledges "innocuous" Twitter conversation with DNC Hackers"; 10 March 2017; https://www.thewashingtontimes.com/news/2017/mar/10/roger-stone-trump-confidant-acknowledges-innocuos/.

[77] ▓▓

[78] ▓▓▓▓▓▓▓▓▓▓▓▓▓▓▓▓▓▓▓▓▓▓▓▓▓▓▓▓▓▓▓▓▓▓▓▓

[79] ▓▓▓▓▓ FBI; FD-302; "Interview of Carter Page"; ▓▓▓▓▓▓ ; 16 March 2017; 16 March 2017; ▓▓▓▓▓▓▓

[80] ▓ Web site; NPR.org; "How the Trump Campaign Weakened the Republic Platform on Aid to Ukraine" 06 August 2016; http://www.npr.org/2016/08/06/488876597/how-the-trump-campagin-weakened-the-republican-platform-on-aid-to-ukraine; accessed 10 November 2016; NPR is an online and media news source.

[81] ▓ Web site; The Daily Beast; "Trump Campaign Changed Ukraine Platform, Lied About it" 03 August 2016; http://www.thedailybeast.com/article/2016/08/03/trump-campaign-changed-Ukraine-platform-lied-about-it.html;accessed 10 November 2016; The Daily Beast is an online and media news source.

[82] ▓ Website; New York Times, "Transcript: Donald Trump on NATO, Turkey's Coup Attempt and the World" 21 July 2016; http://www.nytimes.com/2016/07/22/us/politics/donald-trump-foreign-policy-interview.html

[83] ▓ Web site; Esquire; "How Russia Pulled off the Biggest Election Hack in U.S History" 20 October 2016; http://www.esquire.com/news-politics/a49791/Russian-DNC-emails-hacked;accessed 10 November 2016; Esquire is an online and print news source.

[84] ▓ FBI; EC; ▓▓

[85] ▓ FBI; EC; ▓▓▓▓▓▓▓▓▓▓▓▓▓▓▓▓▓▓▓▓▓▓▓▓▓▓▓▓▓▓▓▓▓▓▓▓▓▓ .

[86] ▓ Web site; The Telegraph; "Exclusive Investigation: Donald Trump Faces Foreign Donor Fundraising Scandal" 24 October 2016; http://www.telegraph.co.uk/news/2016/10/24/exclusive-investigation-donald-Trump-faces-foreign-donor-funrai.html; accessed 14 November 2016; The Telegraph is a British news and media source.

[87] ▓ Web site; CNN; "China's Xi Jinping and Donald Trump Speak after Election Win" 14 November 2016; http://www.cnn.com/2016/11/14/politics/Trump-Xi-Phone-Call/index.html; accessed 14 November 2016; CNN is an online and media news source.

[88] ▓ Web site; Donald J. Trump; "Donald Trump's 7-Point Plan to Rebuild the American Economy by Fighting for Fair Trade" November 2016; http://www.donaldjtrump.com/politics/trade.html; accessed 14 November 2016; Donald J. Trump is a website about the presidential candidate.

[89] ▓ Zachary Mider; Bloomberg News; "Trump's New Russia Advisor has deep ties to Kremlin's Gazprom"; 30 March 2016; ▓ Franklin Foer; Slate; "The Quiet American"; 04 April 2016; ▓ Robert Zubrin; National Review; "Trump: The Kremlin's Candidate"; 4 April 2016; ▓ Michael Isikoff; Yahoo News; "Top Trump Aide Lobbied for Pakistani Spy Front"; 18 April 2016; ▓ Steven Mufson, and Tom Hamburger; "The Washington Post; "Inside Trump advisor Manafort's world of politics and global financial dealmaking"; 26 April 2016; ▓ Leonid Bershidsky; Bloomberg; "Trump's Manager Is a Master of Post-Soviet Business"; 20 July

*Report Date
**Date Report Provided to FBI by Steele

Report Provided to Journalists, Not FBI
Report Not Provided to Corn

2016; ▮ Anna Nemtsova; Politico; "Why Russia is rejoicing over Trump"; 21 July 2016; ▮ Julian Borger; The Guardian; "Putin is surely backing Trump, whether or not Russia was behind DNC Hack"; 25 July 2016.

[90] ▮ Zachary Mider; Bloomberg News; "Trump's New Russia Advisor has deep ties to Kremlin's Gazprom"; 30 March 2016; ▮ Franklin Foer; Slate; "The Quiet American"; 04 April 2016; ▮ Robert Zubrin; National Review; "Trump: The Kremlin's Candidate"; 4 April 2016; ▮ Michael Isikoff; Yahoo News; "Top Trump Aide Lobbied for Pakistani Spy Front"; 18 April 2016; ▮ Steven Mufson, and Tom Hamburger; "The Washington Post; "Inside Trump advisor Manafort's world of politics and global financial dealmaking"; 26 April 2016; ▮ Leonid Bershidsky; Bloomberg; "Trump's Manager Is a Master of Post-Soviet Business"; 20 July 2016; ▮ Anna Nemtsova; Politico; "Why Russia is rejoicing over Trump"; 21 July 2016; ▮ Julian Borger; The Guardian; "Putin is surely backing Trump, whether or not Russia was behind DNC Hack"; 25 July 2016.

[91] ▮ Ivan Nechepurenko; New York Times; "Russian Officials Were in Contact with Trump Allies, Diplomat says"; 10 November 2016; http://nyti.ms/2efpwge

[92] ▮ Michael Crowley; Politico; "When Trump Brought Miss Universe to Moscow"; 15 May 2016.

[93] ▮ Online newspaper article; The Washington Post; "Inside Trump's financial ties to Russia and his unusual flattery of Vladimir Putin"; 17 June 2016; https://www.washingtonpost.com/politics/inside-trumps-financial-ties-to-russia-and-his-unusual-flattery-of-vladimir-putin/2016/06/17/dbdcaac8-31a6-11e6-8ff7-7b6c1998b7a0_story.html.

[94] ▮ FBI; ▮.

[95] ▮ Forbes; "#148 Dmitry Rybolovlev: Net Worth 7.7 Billion"; 22 November 2016; http://www.forbes.com/profile/dmitry-rybolovlev/

[96] ▮ Ivan Nechepurenko; New York Times; "Russian Officials Were in Contact with Trump Allies, Diplomat says"; 10 November 2016; http://nyti.ms/2efpwge

[97] ▮ FBI; ▮.

[98] ▮ Online newspaper article; The Washington Post; "Inside Trump's financial ties to Russia and his unusual flattery of Vladimir Putin"; 17 June 2016; https://www.washingtonpost.com/politics/inside-trumps-financial-ties-to-russia-and-his-unusual-flattery-of-vladimir-putin/2016/06/17/dbdcaac8-31a6-11e6-8ff7-7b6c1998b7a0_story.html.

[99] ▮

[100] ▮

[101] ▮ Oleg Yegorov; Russia Beyond the Headlines; "Russian Intelligence Saved Erdogan from overthrow-media reports"; 21 July 2016

[102] ▮ Zia Wise, Roland Oliphant; The Telegraph; "Erdogan praises 'dear friend' Vladimir Putin in Russian-Turkish Détente"; 9th August 2016

[103] ▮ Emily Sherwin; DW; "Calls for Medvedev's resignation grow louder"; 8 November 2016.

[104] ▮ ; "(U) Kremlin Says Accusing Russia of US Hacker Attacks 'Absurd'"; 28 July 2016; ▮

[105] ▮ ; ▮ ;

[106] ▮ ; "(U) Russian intelligence offers no comment on US hacking claims"; 1 August 2016; ▮

Report Provided to Journalists, Not FBI
Report Not Provided to Corn

SENATE-FISA2020-001663

[107] ▮ "▮ Kremlin Says Accusing Russia of US Hacker Attacks 'Absurd'"; 28 July 2016; ▮

[108] ▮ Oleg Yegorov; Russia Beyond the Headlines; "Russian Intelligence Saved Erdogan from overthrow-media reports"; 21 July 2016

[109] ▮ Emily Sherwin; DW; "Calls for Medvedev's resignation grow louder"; 8 November 2016.

[110] ▮ Online newspaper article; Huffington Post; "The Psychopathology of Donald Trump; 3 August 2016.

[111] ▮ Online newspaper article; Vice; "How Hackers Broke Into John Podesta and Colin Powell's G-mail Accounts"; 20 September 2016; https://www.motherboard.vice.com/read/how-hackers-broke-into-john-podesta-and-colin-powells-gmail-accounts.html; Accessed 22 November 2016.

[112] ▮ Online newspaper article; The Washington Post; "Trump's Russia adviser speaks out, calls accusations 'complete garbage'"; 26 September 2016; https://www.washingtonpost.com/news/josh-rogin/wp/2016/09/26/trumps-russia-adviser-speaks-out-calls-accusations-complete-garbage/.

[113] ▮

[114] ▮ Online newspaper article; The Washington Post; "Trump adviser Michael T. Flynn on his dinner with Putin and why Russia Today is just like CNN"; 15 August 2016; https://www.washingtonpost.com/news/checkpoint/wp/2016/08/15/trump-adviser-michael-t-flynn-on-his-dinner-with-putin-and-why-russia-today-is-just-like-cnn/.

[115] ▮ FBI; FD-302; ▮ 15 February 2017; 24 January 2017; "▮ Michael Flynn"; ▮

[116] ▮ Online news article; CNN; "Former top Trump aide Flynn paid over $30,000 by Russian TV, top house Dem says"; 16 March 2017; www.cnn.com/2017/03/16/politics/michael-flynn-payments-rt-russia-tv; accessed on 5 April 2017.

[117] ▮ Online article; The Daily Beast; "Michael Flynn Failed to Disclose Payments From Russian Propaganda Network"; 1 April 2017; www.thedailybeast.com/articles/2017/04/01/michael-flynn-failed-to-disclose-payments-from-russian-propaganda-network.html; accessed on 5 April 2017.

[118] ▮ Online article; CNN; "Former top Trump aide Flynn paid over $30,000 by Russian TV, top house Dem says"; 16 March 2017; www.cnn.com/2017/03/16/politics/michael-flynn-payments-rt-russia-tv; accessed on 5 April 2017.

[119] ▮ Online article; The Daily Beast; "Michael Flynn Failed to Disclose Payments From Russian Propaganda Network"; 1 April 2017; www.thedailybeast.com/articles/2017/04/01/michael-flynn-failed-to-disclose-payments-from-russian-propaganda-network.html; accessed on 5 April 2017.

[120] ▮ Online article; CNN; "Former top Trump aide Flynn paid over $30,000 by Russian TV, top house Dem says"; 16 March 2017; www.cnn.com/2017/03/16/politics/michael-flynn-payments-rt-russia-tv; accessed on 5 April 2017.

[121] ▮ Online newspaper article; Newsweek; "Dear Donald Trump and Vladimir Putin, I am not Sidney Blumenthal"; 10 October 1016; https://www.newsweek.com/vladimir-putin-sidney-blumenthal-hillary-clinton-donald-trump-benghazi-sputnik-508635.; Accessed 22 November 2016.

[122] ▮ Online newspaper article; Vice; "How Hackers Broke Into John Podesta and Colin Powell's G-mail Accounts"; 20 September 2016; https://www.motherboard.vice.com/read/how-hackers-broke-into-john-podesta-and-colin-powells-gmail-accounts.html; Accessed 22 November 2016.

[123] ▮ Online newspaper article; The Washington Post; "Trump's Russia adviser speaks out, calls accusations 'complete garbage'"; 26 September 2016; https://www.washingtonpost.com/news/josh-rogin/wp/2016/09/26/trumps-russia-adviser-speaks-out-calls-accusations-complete-garbage/.

[124] ▮

[125] ▮ Online newspaper article; The Washington Post; "Trump adviser Michael T. Flynn on his dinner with Putin and why Russia Today is just like CNN"; 15 August 2016; https://www.washingtonpost.com/news/checkpoint/wp/2016/08/15/trump-adviser-michael-t-flynn-on-his-dinner-with-putin-and-why-russia-today-is-just-like-cnn/.

*Report Date

**Date Report Provided to FBI by Steele ▮

Report Provided to Journalists, Not FBI

Report Not Provided to Corn

[126] Website article; Three Way Fight Blog, "The LaRouche Network's Russia Connection"; 03 July 2015; https://www.threewayfight.blogspot.ie/2015/07/the-larouche-networks-russia-connection.html; Accessed on 22 November 2016. Three Way Fight is an online media and blog source.

[127] Online newspaper article; The Washington Post; "Trump adviser Michael T. Flynn on his dinner with Putin and why Russia Today is just like CNN"; 15 August 2016; https://www.washingtonpost.com/news/checkpoint/wp/2016/08/15/trump-adviser-michael-t-flynn-on-his-dinner-with-putin-and-why-russia-today-is-just-like-cnn/.

[128] ██ FBI; FD-302; ██████ 15 February 2017; 24 January 2017; ██████ Michael Flynn"; ██████

[129] Online news article; CNN; "Former top Trump aide Flynn paid over $30,000 by Russian TV, top house Dem says"; 16 March 2017; www.cnn.com/2017/03/16/politics/michael-flynn-payments-rt-russia-tv; accessed on 5 April 2017.

[130] Online article; The Daily Beast; "Michael Flynn Failed to Disclose Payments From Russian Propaganda Network"; 1 April 2017; www.thedailybeast.com/articles/2017/04/01/michael-flynn-failed-to-disclose-payments-from-russian-propaganda-network.html; accessed on 5 April 2017.

[131] Online article; CNN; "Former top Trump aide Flynn paid over $30,000 by Russian TV, top house Dem says"; 16 March 2017; www.cnn.com/2017/03/16/politics/michael-flynn-payments-rt-russia-tv; accessed on 5 April 2017.

[132] Online article; The Daily Beast; "Michael Flynn Failed to Disclose Payments From Russian Propaganda Network"; 1 April 2017; www.thedailybeast.com/articles/2017/04/01/michael-flynn-failed-to-disclose-payments-from-russian-propaganda-network.html; accessed on 5 April 2017.

[133] Online article; CNN; "Former top Trump aide Flynn paid over $30,000 by Russian TV, top house Dem says"; 16 March 2017; www.cnn.com/2017/03/16/politics/michael-flynn-payments-rt-russia-tv; accessed on 5 April 2017.

[134] Website article; The Los Angeles Times, "In Political Turnabout, Democrats Play Soft on Russia Card by Linking Trump to Putin"; 25 July 2016; https://www.latimes.com/politics/la-na-pol-russia-trump-democrats--20160724-snap-story.html; Accessed on 22 November 2016, The LA times is an online and print news source.

[135] Website article; Sputnik News, "When Hillary Clinton Gets Scared She Plays the Russia Card"; 28 September 2016; https://www.sputniknews.com/politics/201609281045806314-Clinton-Trump-Russia-Card/; Accessed on 22 November 2016; Sputnik News is a Russian based online media source.

[136] Website article; The Los Angeles Times, "In Political Turnabout, Democrats Play Soft on Russia Card by Linking Trump to Putin"; 25 July 2016; https://www.latimes.com/politics/la-na-pol-russia-trump-democrats--20160724-snap-story.html; Accessed on 22 November 2016, The LA times is an online and print news source.

[137] Website article; Sputnik News, "When Hillary Clinton Gets Scared She Plays the Russia Card"; 28 September 2016; https://www.sputniknews.com/politics/201609281045806314-Clinton-Trump-Russia-Card/; Accessed on 22 November 2016; Sputnik News is a Russian based online media source.

[138] Online news article; New York Times; "Secret Ledger in Ukraine Lists Cash for Donald Trump's Campaign Chief"; 14 August 2016; Source is a US media outlet.

[139] ████████████

[140] *R███████
**Date Report Provided to FBI by Steele

Report Provided to Journalists, Not FBI
Report Not Provided to Corn

SENATE-FISA2020-001665

141

142 Online news article; New York Times; "Secret Ledger in Ukraine Lists Cash for Donald Trump's Campaign Chief"; 14 August 2016; Source is a US media outlet.

143

144

145 Online news article; New York Times; "Secret Ledger in Ukraine Lists Cash for Donald Trump's Campaign Chief"; 14 August 2016; Source is a US media outlet.

146

147

148

150

151 Web site; Kremlin.ru; "Meeting with Sergei Ivanov and Anton Vaino"; 12 August 2016; en.kremlin.ru/events/president/news/52691.

152

153

154 Web site; Kremlin.ru; "Meeting with Sergei Ivanov and Anton Vaino"; 12 August 2016; en.kremlin.ru/events/president/news/52691.

155

156

157 Web site; dw.com; "Putin denies plans to 'influence' US elections"; 16 October 2016; www.dw.come/en/putin-denies-plans-to-influence-us-election/a-36055691; 01 December 2016.

158 Web site; Politifact.com; "Hillary Clinton flip-flops on Trans-Pacific Partnership"; 08 October 2016; www.politifact.com/truth-o-meter/statemetns/2015/oct/08/hillary-clinton/hillary-clinton-now-opposes-trans-pacific-partners/; 01 December 2016; Source is a political fact checking website.

*Report Date
**Date Report Provided to FBI by Steele

Report Provided to Journalists, Not FBI
Report Not Provided to Corn

SENATE-FISA2020-001666

[159] ▉ Web site; Politifact.com; "Hillary Clinton flip-flops on Trans-Pacific Partnership"; 08 October 2016; www.politifact.com/truth-o-meter/statemetns/2015/oct/08/hillary-clinton/hillary-clinton-now-opposes-trans-pacific-partners/; 01 December 2016; Source is a political fact checking website.

[160] ▉ Web site; Politifact.com; "Hillary Clinton flip-flops on Trans-Pacific Partnership"; 08 October 2016; www.politifact.com/truth-o-meter/statemetns/2015/oct/08/hillary-clinton/hillary-clinton-now-opposes-trans-pacific-partners/; 01 December 2016; Source is a political fact checking website.

[161] ▉ Web site; Politifact.com; "Hillary Clinton flip-flops on Trans-Pacific Partnership"; 08 October 2016; www.politifact.com/truth-o-meter/statemetns/2015/oct/08/hillary-clinton/hillary-clinton-now-opposes-trans-pacific-partners/; 01 December 2016; Source is a political fact checking website.

[162] ▉ Web site; wikileaks.org; "TPP Treaty: Intellectual Property Rights Chapter, Consolidated Text (October 5, 2015)"; 09 October 2015; https://wikileaks.org/tpp-ip3/wikileaks-tpp-ip-chapter/wikileaks-tpp-ip-chapter-051015.pdf; 01 December 2016; Source is a leaker site likely used as a propaganda tool by the Kremlin to leak real or altered classified documents.

[163] ▉ Web site; Politifact.com; "Hillary Clinton flip-flops on Trans-Pacific Partnership"; 08 October 2016; www.politifact.com/truth-o-meter/statemetns/2015/oct/08/hillary-clinton/hillary-clinton-now-opposes-trans-pacific-partners/; 01 December 2016; Source is a political fact checking website.

[164] ▉ Web site; Politifact.com; "Hillary Clinton flip-flops on Trans-Pacific Partnership"; 08 October 2016; www.politifact.com/truth-o-meter/statemetns/2015/oct/08/hillary-clinton/hillary-clinton-now-opposes-trans-pacific-partners/; 01 December 2016; Source is a political fact checking website.

[165] ▉ Web site; Politifact.com; "Hillary Clinton flip-flops on Trans-Pacific Partnership"; 08 October 2016; www.politifact.com/truth-o-meter/statemetns/2015/oct/08/hillary-clinton/hillary-clinton-now-opposes-trans-pacific-partners/; 01 December 2016; Source is a political fact checking website.

[166] ▉ Web site; cbsnews.com; "Leaked emails show slogans Clinton campaign considered"; www.cbsnews.com/news/leaked-podesta-emails-show-clinton-campaign-slogans-considered-tpp-stance/; 01 December 2016; CBS news is an American news site.

[167] ▉ Web site; breitbart.com; "Wikileaks: Soros memo accused Obama of fueling radical Islam to push TPP"; 24 October 2016; www.breitbart.com/national-security/2016/10/24/wikileaks-soros-sent-john-podesta-memo-showing-obama-supported-radical-islam-push-tpp/; 01 December 2016; Breitbart is headed by Trump's advisor and alt-right activist.

[168] ▉ Web site; JKL Newsroom; 26 May 2016; "Positions: Where are the candidates on TTIP?" jklnewsroom.com/index.php/2016/05/26/candidates-on-ttip/; 01 December 2016; JKL Newsroom is Swedish company with an American analyst who served on Obama's 2012 campaign and Emanuel's 2015 re-election campaign.

[169] ▉ Web site; ballotpedia.org; "2016 Presidential Candidates on International Trade"; https://ballotpedia.org/2016_presidential_candidates_on_international_trade; Source is an encyclopedia of American politics.

[170] ▉ Web site; ballotpedia.org; "2016 Presidential Candidates on International Trade"; https://ballotpedia.org/2016_presidential_candidates_on_international_trade; Source is an encyclopedia of American politics.

[171] ▉ Web site; ballotpedia.org; "2016 Presidential Candidates on International Trade"; https://ballotpedia.org/2016_presidential_candidates_on_international_trade; Source is an encyclopedia of American politics.

*Report Date

**Date Report Provided to FBI by ▉Steele▉

Report Provided to Journalists, Not FBI

Report Not Provided to Corn

[172] Web site; ballotpedia.org; "2016 Presidential Candidates on International Trade"; https://ballotpedia.org/2016_presidential_candidates _on_international_trade; Source is an encyclopedia of American politics.

[173] Web site; ballotpedia.org; "2016 Presidential Candidates on International Trade"; https://ballotpedia.org/2016_presidential_candidates _on_international_trade; Source is an encyclopedia of American politics.

[174] Web site; ballotpedia.org; "2016 Presidential Candidates on International Trade"; https://ballotpedia.org/2016_presidential_candidates _on_international_trade; Source is an encyclopedia of American politics.

[175] Web site; JKL Newsroom; 26 May 2016; "Positions: Where are the candidates on TTIP?" jklnewsroom.com/index.php/2016/05/26/candidates-on-ttip/; 01 December 2016; JKL Newsroom is Swedish company with an American analyst who served on Obama's 2012 campaign and Emanuel's 2015 re-election campaign.

[176] Web site; breitbart.com; 13 October 2016; "Team Trump on explosive WikiLeaks Clinton TPP emails: 'reveals' Hilary really supports deal, 'lied' to public"; www.breitbart.com/big-government/2016/10/13/team-trump-explosive-wikileaks-clinton-tpp-emails-reveals-hillary-really-supports-deal-lied-public/; 01 December 2016; Breitbart is headed by Trump's advisor and alt-right activist.

[177]

[178]

[179]

[180]

[181]

[182]

[183]

[184]

[185] Web site; Kremlin.ru; "Meeting with Sergei Ivanov and Anton Vaino"; 12 August 2016; en.kremlin.ru/events/president/news/52691.

[186]

[187] Web site; Kremlin.ru; "Meeting with Sergei Ivanov and Anton Vaino"; 12 August 2016; en.kremlin.ru/events/president/news/52691.

[188]

[189] Twitter; Wikileaks Twitter Feed" 07 October 2016;

*Report Date
**Date Report Provided to FBI by Steele

Report Provided to Journalists, Not FBI
Report Not Provided to Corn

SENATE-FISA2020-001668

[190] ██

[191] ██ Website article; The Los Angeles Times, "In Political Turnabout, Democrats Play Soft on Russia Card by Linking Trump to Putin"; 25 July 2016; https://www.latimes.com/politics/la-na-pol-russia-trump-democrats--20160724-snap-story.html; Accessed on 22 November 2016, The LA times is an online and print news source.

[192] ██ Website article; Sputnik News, "When Hillary Clinton Gets Scared She Plays the Russia Card"; 28 September 2016; https://www.sputniknews.com/politics/201609281045806314-Clinton-Trump-Russia-Card/; Accessed on 22 November 2016; Sputnik News is a Russian based online media source.

[193] ██

[194] ██ Web site; dw.com; "Putin denies plans to 'influence' US elections"; 16 October 2016; www.dw.come/en/putin-denies-plans-to-influence-us-election/a-36055691; 01 December 2016.

[195] ██ Web site; Politifact.com; "Hillary Clinton flip-flops on Trans-Pacific Partnership"; 08 October 2016; www.politifact.com/truth-o-meter/statemetns/2015/oct/08/hillary-clinton/hillary-clinton-now-opposes-trans-pacific-partners/; 01 December 2016; Source is a political fact checking website.

[196] ██ Web site; Politifact.com; "Hillary Clinton flip-flops on Trans-Pacific Partnership"; 08 October 2016; www.politifact.com/truth-o-meter/statemetns/2015/oct/08/hillary-clinton/hillary-clinton-now-opposes-trans-pacific-partners/; 01 December 2016; Source is a political fact checking website.

[197] ██ Web site; Politifact.com; "Hillary Clinton flip-flops on Trans-Pacific Partnership"; 08 October 2016; www.politifact.com/truth-o-meter/statemetns/2015/oct/08/hillary-clinton/hillary-clinton-now-opposes-trans-pacific-partners/; 01 December 2016; Source is a political fact checking website.

[198] ██ Web site; Politifact.com; "Hillary Clinton flip-flops on Trans-Pacific Partnership"; 08 October 2016; www.politifact.com/truth-o-meter/statemetns/2015/oct/08/hillary-clinton/hillary-clinton-now-opposes-trans-pacific-partners/; 01 December 2016; Source is a political fact checking website.

[199] ██ Web site; wikileaks.org; "TPP Treaty: Intellectual Property Rights Chapter, Consolidated Text (October 5, 2015)"; 09 October 2015; https://wikileaks.org/tpp-ip3/wikileaks-tpp-ip-chapter/wikileaks-tpp-ip-chapter-051015.pdf; 01 December 2016; Source is a leaker site likely used as a propaganda tool by the Kremlin to leak real or altered classified documents.

[200] ██ Web site; Politifact.com; "Hillary Clinton flip-flops on Trans-Pacific Partnership"; 08 October 2016; www.politifact.com/truth-o-meter/statemetns/2015/oct/08/hillary-clinton/hillary-clinton-now-opposes-trans-pacific-partners/; 01 December 2016; Source is a political fact checking website.

[201] ██ Web site; Politifact.com; "Hillary Clinton flip-flops on Trans-Pacific Partnership"; 08 October 2016; www.politifact.com/truth-o-meter/statemetns/2015/oct/08/hillary-clinton/hillary-clinton-now-opposes-trans-pacific-partners/; 01 December 2016; Source is a political fact checking website.

*Report Date
**Date Report Provided to FBI by Steele

Report Provided to Journalists, Not FBI
Report Not Provided to Corn

[202] ██ Web site; Politifact.com; "Hillary Clinton flip-flops on Trans-Pacific Partnership"; 08 October 2016; www.politifact.com/truth-o-meter/statemetns/2015/oct/08/hillary-clinton/hillary-clinton-now-opposes-trans-pacific-partners/; 01 December 2016; Source is a political fact checking website.

[203] ██ Web site; cbsnews.com; "Leaked emails show slogans Clinton campaign considered"; www.cbsnews.com/news/leaked-podesta-emails-show-clinton-campaign-slogans-considered-tpp-stance/; 01 December 2016; CBS news is an American news site.

[204] ██ Web site; breitbart.com; "Wikileaks: Soros memo accused Obama of fueling radical Islam to push TPP"; 24 October 2016; www.breitbart.com/national-security/2016/10/24/wikileaks-soros-sent-john-podesta-memo-showing-obama-supported-radical-islam-push-tpp/; 01 December 2016; Breitbart is headed by Trump's advisor and alt-right activist.

[205] ██ Web site; JKL Newsroom; 26 May 2016; "Positions: Where are the candidates on TTIP?" jklnewsroom.com/index.php/2016/05/26/candidates-on-ttip/; 01 December 2016; JKL Newsroom is Swedish company with an American analyst who served on Obama's 2012 campaign and Emanuel's 2015 re-election campaign.

[206] ██ Web site; ballotpedia.org; "2016 Presidential Candidates on International Trade"; https://ballotpedia.org/2016_presidential_candidates_on_international_trade; Source is an encyclopedia of American politics.

[207] ██ Web site; ballotpedia.org; "2016 Presidential Candidates on International Trade"; https://ballotpedia.org/2016_presidential_candidates_on_international_trade; Source is an encyclopedia of American politics.

[208] ██ Web site; ballotpedia.org; "2016 Presidential Candidates on International Trade"; https://ballotpedia.org/2016_presidential_candidates_on_international_trade; Source is an encyclopedia of American politics.

[209] ██ Web site; ballotpedia.org; "2016 Presidential Candidates on International Trade"; https://ballotpedia.org/2016_presidential_candidates_on_international_trade; Source is an encyclopedia of American politics.

[210] ██ Web site; ballotpedia.org; "2016 Presidential Candidates on International Trade"; https://ballotpedia.org/2016_presidential_candidates_on_international_trade; Source is an encyclopedia of American politics.

[211] ██ Web site; ballotpedia.org; "2016 Presidential Candidates on International Trade"; https://ballotpedia.org/2016_presidential_candidates_on_international_trade; Source is an encyclopedia of American politics.

[212] ██ Web site; JKL Newsroom; 26 May 2016; "Positions: Where are the candidates on TTIP?" jklnewsroom.com/index.php/2016/05/26/candidates-on-ttip/; 01 December 2016; JKL Newsroom is Swedish company with an American analyst who served on Obama's 2012 campaign and Emanuel's 2015 re-election campaign.

[213] ██ Web site; breitbart.com; 13 October 2016; "Team Trump on explosive WikiLeaks Clinton TPP emails: 'reveals' Hilary really supports deal, 'lied' to public"; www.breitbart.com/big-government/2016/10/13/team-trump-explosive-wikileaks-clinton-tpp-emails-reveals-hillary-really-supports-deal-lied-public/; 01 December 2016; Breitbart is headed by Trump's advisor and alt-right activist.

[214] ████████████████████

[215] ████████████████████

[216] ██ FBI; ████████

[217] ██ ; "(U) Australia: Hotline to Moscow bank revealed as FBI probes Kremlin's five-year Trump plan"; 01 November 2016; ████

*Report Date
**Date Report Provided to FBI by Steele

Report Provided to Journalists, Not FBI
Report Not Provided to Corn

PRODUCED TO SJC/SSCI

[218] ██████ ALFA GROUP DROPS SLOBODIN FROM SUPERVISORY BOARDCITE OSC RESTON VA 502688"; 09 September 2016; ██████

[219] ████ " Australia: Hotline to Moscow bank revealed as FBI probes Kremlin's five-year Trump plan"; 01 November 2016; ██████

[220] ██████

[221] ██████

[222] ██████

[223] "Biography of Russian president's new representative in Central Federal District"; 06 September 2011; ██████

[224] ██ Online news article; Sputnik news; "Putin Signs Law to Crack Down on Offshore Tax Shelters"; 25 November 2014; https://sputniknews.com/russia/201411251015135980/; 01 December 2016; Sputnik International is a Kremlin sponsored international news agency.

[225] ██ Online news article; Sputnik news; "Everyone's a winner as Russian banks and European savers team up"; 02 June 2015; https://sputniknews.com/russia/201411251015135980/; 01 December 2016; Sputnik International is a Kremlin sponsored international news agency.

[226] ██████

[227] █ RUSSIAN CORRUPTION CASES SEEN POSSIBLY TARGETING OLIGARCHS Vekselberg, Fridman ██████ 14 September 2016; ██████

[228] ██████

[229] ██████

[230] ██████

[231] ██████

[232] ██████) Biographical Details of New Russian Minister of Regional Development" 22 May 2012. Online news article; Sputnik News; "Russian Regional Development Minister to Resign - Forbes"; 26 September 2016; https://sputniknews.com/russia/20120926176230659; Sputnik International is a Kremlin sponsored international news agency.

[233] ██ Online news article; Sputnik News; "Busy Schedule Precludes Putin's Visit to Memorial Service for Karimov"; 03 September 2016; Sputnik International is a Kremlin sponsored international news agency.

[234] ██ Online news article; Indian Express; "Vladimir Putin lays flowers at Uzbek strongman Islam Karimov's grave"; 06 September 2016; indaiexpress.com/article/world-news/Vladimir-putin-lays-flowers-at-uzbek-stronman-islam-karimovs-grave/

[235] ██████ " ██████ - ENGLISH) Biographical Details Of New Russian Minister Of Regional Development" 22 May 2012.

[236] ██████; ██████ - ENGLISH) Biographical Details Of New Russian Minister Of Regional Development" 22 May 2012.

[237] ██ Online news article; Sputnik News; "Rosneft Signs Deal to Buy AAR's Half-Share of TNK-BF"; 12 December 2012; Sputnik International is a Kremlin sponsored international news agency.

[238] Steele Reporting- 18 October 2016

*Re████ Date

**Date Report Provided to FBI by Steele

Report Provided to Journalists, Not FBI
Report Not Provided to Corn

[239] Steele Reporting- 18 October 2016

[240] Steele Reporting- 18 October 2016

[241] http://missuniverse.com/theshow/index/year:2013

[242] Steele Reporting- 18 October 2016

[243] Steele Reporting- 18 October 2016

[244] ███ FBI; ████████████████████

[245] http://www.ritzcarlton.com/en/hotels/europe/moscow/rooms-suites

[246] http://ritzcarlton.com/en/hotels/europe/moscow/hotel-overview/press-releases/renovated-presidential-suite

[247] Pravda; ""Barack Obama to stay at 13,000-dollar luxury suite at Moscow's Ritz-Carlton Hotel"; 3 July 2009.

[248] ██████████) FBI; ██████████████████████████

[249] http://eng.crocus-expo.ru/exhibitioncenter/

[250] Steele Reporting- 18 October 2016

[251] Steele Reporting- 18 October 2016

[252] http://crocusgroup.com/objects

[253] Steele Reporting- 18 October 2016

[254] Ibid.

[255] Steele Reporting- 18 October 2016

[256] Michael Crowely; Politico; "When Donald Trump Brought Miss Universe to Moscow"; 15 May 2016; http://www.politico.com/story/2016/05/donald-trump-russia-moscow-miss-universe-223173

[257] Tom Hamburger, Rosalind S. Helderman, and Michael Birnbaum; Washington Post; "Inside Trump's Financial ties to Russia and his unusual flattery of Vladimir Putin"; 17 June 2016; https://www.washingtonpost.com/politics/inside-trumps-financial-ties-to-russia-and-his-unusual-flattery-of-vladimir-putin/2016/06/17

[258] Steele Reporting- 18 October 2016

[259] Russ Choma; Mother Jones; "Donald Trump is Doing Business with a Controversial Azerbaijani Oligarch"; 29 July 2015; http://www.motherjones.com/politics/2015/07/donald-trump-azerbaijan-anar-mammadov

[260] Steele Reporting- 18 October 2016

[261] http://www.ivankatrump.com/tag/baku ; and

[262] Steele Reporting- 18 October 2016

[263] Crowely, "When Donald Trump Brought Miss Universe to Moscow; Hamburger; "Inside Trump's financial ties to Russia and his unusual flattery of Vladimir Putin."

[264] Steele Reporting- 18 October 2016

[265] Russ Choma; Mother Jones; "Donald Trump is Doing Business with a Controversial Azerbaijani Oligarch"; 29 July 2015; http://www.motherjones.com/politics/2015/07/donald-trump-azerbaijan-anar-mammadov

[266] Steele Reporting- 18 October 2016

*R███ Date

**Date Report Provided to FBI by Steele

Report Provided to Journalists, Not FBI
Report Not Provided to Corn

PRODUCED TO SJC/SSCI

267 ▮ Meydan TV; "Leyla Aliyeva and Emin Agalarov's announce split via Instagram"; 31 May 2015; http://meydan.tv/en/site/news/6130/leyla-aliyeva-and-emin-agalarov-announce-split-via-instgram.htm

268 ▮ En.president.az

269 Steele Reporting- 18 October 2016

270 ▮ https://www.youtube.com/watch?v=iuzunjfs658

271 Steele Reporting- 18 October 2016

272 ▮ Russ Choma; Mother Jones; "Donald Trump is Doing Business with a Controversial Azerbaijani Oligarch"; 29 July 2015; http://www.motherjones.com/politics/2015/07/donald-trump-azerbaijan-anar-mammadov

273 ▮ Scott Higham, Steven Rich and Alice Crites; Washington Post; "10 members of Congress took trip secretly funded by foreign government"; 13 May 2015; http://www.washingtonpost.com/investigations/10-members-of-congress-took-trip-secretly-funded-by-foreign-government/2015/05

274 ▮ http://www.anarmammadov.com/news/azerbaijan-america-alliance-hosted-its-3rd-annual-gala-dinner

275 ▮ FBI; ▮

276 ▮ FBI; ▮

277 ▮

278 ▮

279 ▮

280 ▮

281 ▮ Online news article; Yahoo.com; "U.S. intel officials probe ties between Trump adviser and Kremlin"; 23 September 2016; https://www.yahoo.com/news/u-s-intel-officials-probe-ties-between-trump-adviser-and-kremlin-175046002.html; accessed on 9 November 2016; Yahoo.com is the owner of Yahoo! News, an aggregator of news. The article is based on reporting from a senior US law enforcement Western intelligence source.

282 ▮

283 ▮

284 ▮ https://www.hse.ru.en/

285 ▮ Online news article; Guardian.com; "Trumps foreign policy adviser will talk about his foreign policy – just not today"; 7 July 2016; https://theguardian.com/world/2016/jul/07/carter-page-donald-trump-foreign-policy-advisor-russia; accessed on 9 November 2016; The Guardian is an online public news source.

286 ▮ FBI; FD-302; "Interview of Carter Page"; ▮ 09 March 2017; 21 March 2017; ▮.

287 ▮ Web site; Spiegel Online; "Russia Didn't Initiate the Ukraine Crisis"" 02 September 2014; http://www.spiegel.de/international/business/rosneft-head-igor-sechin-speaks-about-sanctions-and-ukraine-a-989267.html; accessed 21 November 2016; Spiegel Online is a German online media source.

288 ▮ Web site; Bloomberg.com; "Trump's New Russia Adviser Has Deep Ties to Kremlin's Gazprom"; 30 March, 2016; http://www.bloomberg.com/politics/articles/2016-03-30/trump-russia-advisor-carter-page-interview; accessed 15 November 2016; Bloomberg is a business and financial markets public news source.

289 ▮ Web site; Huffingtonpost.com; "A Trump Adviser Once Compares Sanctions Against Russia to Police Killing Black Men"; 21 June 2016; https://www.huffingtonpost.com/entry/trump-carter-page-russia-sanctions-black-lives_us_5769bf64e4b065534f482504; accessed on 15 November 2016; Huffington Post is an online public news source.

*Report Date

**Date Report Provided to FBI by Steele ▮

Report Provided to Journalists, Not FBI
Report Not Provided to Corn

[290] ▮ Josh Nathan-Kazis; Forward; "Meet Michael Cohen, Donald Trump's Jewish Wingman"; 20 July 2015; http://forward.com/news/312123/meet-michael-cohen-donald-trumps-jewish-wingman/

[291] ▮ https://erictrumpfoundation.com/board-of-directors/michael-d.-cohen

[292] ▮ Paul Alexander; The Daily Beast; "Meet Donald Trump's Karl Rove, Michael Cohen"; 21 March 2011; http://www.thedailybeast.com/articles/2011/03/21/meet-donald-

[293] ▮ https://erictrumpfoundation.com/board-of-directors/michael-d.-cohen

[294] ▮ Paul Alexander; The Daily Beast; "Meet Donald Trump's Karl Rove, Michael Cohen"; 21 March 2011; http://www.thedailybeast.com/articles/2011/03/21/meet-donald-

[295] ▮▮▮▮▮▮▮▮▮▮▮▮▮▮▮▮▮▮▮▮▮▮▮▮▮▮▮▮

[296] ▮ Josh Nathan-Kazis; Forward; "Meet Michael Cohen, Donald Trump's Jewish Wingman"; 20 July 2015; http://forward.com/news/312123/meet-michael-cohen-donald-trumps-jewish-wingman/

[297] ▮ Online news article; RFERL.org; "Russia: Consumers Clamor To Buy Luxury Goods"; 1 June 2007; www.rferl.org/a/1076857.html; accessed on 30 November 2016; RFERL is a new reporting company focused on journalism for countries where free press is banned or not fully established.

[298] ▮ Online news article; NY Times; "In Russia, Exile in Comfort for Leaders Like Assad"; 28 December 2012; www.nytimes.com/2012/12/29/world/europe/in-barvikha-russia-leades-like-assad-find-haven.html?r=0&exprod=myyahoo; accessed on 30 November 2016; NY Times is an established source of news based in New York.

[299] ▮ Web site; blv.ru; "About"; https://www.blv.ru/eng/about; accessed on 30 November 2016; BLV is the official web site for the Barvikha Luxury Village.

[300] ▮▮▮▮▮▮▮▮▮▮▮▮▮▮▮▮▮▮▮▮▮▮▮▮▮▮

[301] ▮ ▮ "▮▮▮▮) Putin's Reshuffles: New Blood and Possible Successors"; 27 September 2016;

[302] ▮ Roland Oliphant; The Telegraph; "Shock in the Kremlin as Putin fires Chief of Staff Sergei Ivanov"; 12 August 2016.

[303] Mikhail Klimentyev; TASS; "Putin has appointed Sergei Kiriyenko, the first Deputy Head of the Presidential Administration."; 12 September 2016.

[304] ▮▮▮▮▮▮▮▮▮▮▮▮▮▮▮▮▮▮▮▮▮▮▮▮▮

[305] ▮ Josh Nathan-Kazis; Forward; "Meet Michael Cohen, Donald Trump's Jewish Wingman"; 20 July 2015; http://forward.com/news/312123/meet-michael-cohen-donald-trumps-jewish-wingman/

[306] ▮ https://erictrumpfoundation.com/board-of-directors/michael-d.-cohen

[307] ▮ Paul Alexander; The Daily Beast; "Meet Donald Trump's Karl Rove, Michael Cohen"; 21 March 2011; http://www.thedailybeast.com/articles/2011/03/21/meet-donald-

[308] ▮ https://erictrumpfoundation.com/board-of-directors/michael-d.-cohen

[309] ▮ Paul Alexander; The Daily Beast; "Meet Donald Trump's Karl Rove, Michael Cohen"; 21 March 2011; http://www.thedailybeast.com/articles/2011/03/21/meet-donald-

[310] ▮ Nolan D. McCaskill, Alex Isenstadt, and Shane Goldmacher; Politico; "Paul Manafort Resigns from Trump Campaign"; 19 August 2016.

*R ▮ No Date ▮ ▮ ▮ Report Provided to Journalists, Not FBI
**Date Report Provided to FBI by Steele

Report Not Provided to Corn

PRODUCED TO SJC/SSCI

[311] ▮ Jim Acosta, and Jeremy Diamond; CNN; "Paul Manafort Named campaign chairman, chief strategist for Donald Trump"; 19 May 2016; http://www.cnn.com/2016/05/19/politics/paul-manafort-donald-trump-campaign-chairman/

[312] ▮ Jim Acosta, and Jeremy Diamond; CNN; "Paul Manafort Named campaign chairman, chief strategist for Donald Trump"; 19 May 2016; http://www.cnn.com/2016/05/19/politics/paul-manafort-donald-trump-campaign-chairman/

[313] ▮ Alexander Burns, and Maggie Haberman; The New York Times; "Donald Trump Hires Paul Manafort to Lead Delegate Effort"; 28 March 2016; http://www.nytimes.com/politics/first-draft/2016/03/28/donald-trump-hires-paul-manafort-to-lead-delegate-effort/

-NYT

[314] ▮ Franklin Foer; Slate; "The Quiet American"; 04 April 2016; http://www.slate.com/articles/news_and_politics/politics/2016/04/paul_manafort_isn_t_a_gop_retread_he_s_made_a_career_of_reinventing_tyrants.html

[315] ███

[316] ▮ Andrew E. Kramer, Mike McIntire, and Barry Meier; The New York Times; "Secret Ledger in Ukraine Lists Cash for Donald Trump's Campaign Chief"; 15 August 2016; http://www.nytimes.com/2016/08/15/us/politics/paul-manafort-ukraine-donald-trump.html?_r=0

[317] ▮ FBI; FD-302; ███████████ 02 September 2014; 30 July 2014; ▮ "Interview of Paul Manafort";

[318] ▮ Steven Lee Myers, and Andrew E. Kramer; The New York Times; "How Paul Manafort Wielded Power in Ukraine Before Advising Donald Trump"; 31 July 2016; http://www.nytimes.com/2016/08/01/us/paul-manafort-ukraine-donald-trump.html

[319] ▮ Op. cit., endnote 4

[320] ▮ Leonid Bershidsky; Bloomberg; "Trump's Manager Is a Master of Post-Soviet Business"; 20 July 2016; https://www.bloomberg.com/view/articles/2016-07-20/trump-s-manager-is-a-master-of-post-soviet-business

[321] ▮ Luke Harding; The Guardian; "How Trump's Campaign Chief got a strongman elected president of Ukraine"; 16 August 2016; https://www.theguardian.com/us-news/2016/aug/16/donald-trump-campaign-paul-manafort-ukraine-yanukovich

[322] ▮ Steven Mufson, and Tom Hamburger; The Washington Post; "Inside Trump advisor Manafort's world of politics and global financial dealmaking"; 26 April 2016; https://www.washingtonpost.com/politics/in-business-as-in-politics-trump-adviser-no-stranger-to-controversial-figures/2016/04/26/970db232-08c7-11e6-b283-e79d81c63c1b_story.html

[323] ▮ Op. cit., endnote 5.

[324] ▮ Op. cit., endnote 5.
▮▮ ▮ Op. cit., endnote 4.

*Re█ ██████
**Date Report Provided to FBI by ▮Steele▮

Report Provided to Journalists, Not FBI
Report Not Provided to Corn

[326] ████ FBI; FD-302; ████████████████████; 18 September 2014; 09 July 2014; ██ "Interview of Richard Gates"; ████████

[327] ██ Aleksandra Kharchenko; PolitiFact; "Paul Manafort, Donald Trump's top adviser, and his ties to pro-Russian politicians in Ukraine"; 02 May 2016; http://www.politifact.com/global-news/article/2016/may/02/paul-manafort-donald-trumps-top-adviser-and-his-ti/

[328] ██ Andrew E. Kramer, Mike McIntire, and Barry Meier; The New York Times; "Secret Ledger in Ukraine Lists Cash for Donald Trump's Campaign Chief"; 15 August 2016; http://www.nytimes.com/2016/08/15/us/politics/paul-manafort-ukraine-donald-trump.html?_r=0

[329] ██ David, Wright; CNN; "Manafort named in Ukrainian Probe into Millions of Secret Cash"; 15 August 2016; http://www.cnn.com/2016/08/15/politics/clinton-slams-trump-over-manafort-report/

[330] ██ Graham, David A; The Atlantic; "The Manafort Dossier"; 15 August 2016; http://www.theatlantic.com/politics/archive/2016/08/the-manafort-dossier/495851/

[331] ██ Luke Harding; The Guardian; "How Trump's Campaign Chief got a strongman elected president of Ukraine"; 16 August 2016; https://www.theguardian.com/us-news/2016/aug/16/donald-trump-campaign-paul-manafort-ukraine-yanukovich

[332] ██ FBI; Electronic Communication; ████████████████ 13 January 2016; ██ "Opening EC"; ████████

[333] ██ Bill Chappell; NPR; "How Ukraine's Presidential Documents Got Online So Fast"; 27 February 2014; http://www.npr.org/sections/thetwo-way/2014/02/25/282659892/how-ukraine-s-presidential-documents-got-online-so-fast

[334] ██ *Op. cit.,* endnote 5.

[335] ██ Andrew E. Kramer, Mike McIntire, and Barry Meier; The New York Times; "Secret Ledger in Ukraine Lists Cash for Donald Trump's Campaign Chief"; 15 August 2016; http://www.nytimes.com/2016/08/15/us/politics/paul-manafort-ukraine-donald-trump.html?_r=0

[336] ██ David, Wright; CNN; "Manafort named in Ukrainian Probe into Millions of Secret Cash"; 15 August 2016; http://www.cnn.com/2016/08/15/politics/clinton-slams-trump-over-manafort-report/

[337] ██ Graham, David A; The Atlantic; "The Manafort Dossier"; 15 August 2016; http://www.theatlantic.com/politics/archive/2016/08/the-manafort-dossier/495851/

[338] ██ Jeff Horwitz and Desmond Butler; Associated Press; "Manafort Tied to Undisclosed Foreign Lobbying"; 17 August 2016; http://bigstory.ap.org/article/c01989a47ee5421593ba1b301ec07813/ap-sources-manafort-tied-undisclosed-foreign-lobbying

[339] ██ Nick Glass; Politico; "Scandals Around Trump aide Manafort deepen'; 17 August 2016; http://www.politico.com/story/2016/08/paul-manafort-still-campaign-chairman-227112

[340] ██ http://government.ru/ZSSOZ/EN/Department/200/

[341] ██

[342] ██ Roland Oliphant; The Telegraph; "Shock in the Kremlin as Putin fires Chief of Staff Sergei Ivanov"; 12 August 2016.

[343] Mikhail Klimentyev; TASS; "Putin has appointed Sergei Kiriyenko, the first Deputy Head of the Presidential Administration."; 12 September 2016.

[344] ██

vided to Journalists, Not FBI
Report Not Provided to Corn

**Date Report Provided to FBI by Steele

PRODUCED TO SJC/SSCI

345

346

347

348

349

350

351

352 Lorenzo Piccio; Devex; "Konstantin Kosachev: A change of course for Russian Foreign aid"; 4 December 2014.
353 Lorenzo Piccio; Devex; "Konstantin Kosachev: A change of course for Russian Foreign aid"; 4 December 2014.
354

355 Lorenzo Piccio; Devex; "Konstantin Kosachev: A change of course for Russian Foreign aid"; 4 December 2014.
356 RusskiyMir; "Konstantin Kosachev Appointed Head of Rossotrudnichestvo"; 3 June 2012; http://www.russkiymir.ru/en/news/128251
357

358 Michael Isikov; Yahoo News; "Us Intel officials probe ties between Trump adviser and Kremlin"; 23 September 2016.
359 Tatyana Stanyovaya; Carnegie Moscow Center; "Kremlin-Duma Reshuffle offers false hope to Russian reformers"; 10 October 2016.
360 http://www.gazeta.ru/politics/2015/03/23_a_6611137.shtml
361 Ekaterina Grobman; Russia Beyond the Headlines; "Vyacheslav Volodin: Could the new State Duma speaker be the next president?"; 6 October 2016; http://rbth.com/politics_and_society/2016/10/06/vyacheslav-volodin-could-the-new-state-duma-speaker-be-the-next-president
362 Michael Isikov; Yahoo News; "Us Intel officials probe ties between Trump adviser and Kremlin"; 23 September 2016.
363 United Nations; Treaty; "Vienna Convention on Diplomatic Relations"; Written on 18 April 1961 and ratified on 24 April 1964; Treaty Series, Vol. 500 P. 95
364 Bob Patterson; The Guardian; "US Embassy Cables: Andrei Lugovoi gets new job in Russia's Parliament"; 18 September 2007.
365 Online newspaper article; *The Daily Beast*; "Meet The Man Who Is Spinning For Donald Trump In Russia"; 8 September 2016; https://www.thdailybeast.com/articles/2016/09/08/meet-the-man-who-spinning-for-donald-trump-in-russia.html; accessed on 13 September 2016; *The Daily Beast* is an online news outlet.

*Report Date
**Date Report Provided to FBI by Steele

Report Provided to Journalists, Not FBI
Report Not Provided to Corn

PRODUCED TO SJC/SSCI

[366] ■ Online newspaper article; *ABC News*; "DNC Hack Prompts Questions About Trump's Ties to Russia"; 26 July 2016; https://abcnews.go.com/Politics/dnc-hack-prompts-questions-trumps-ties-russia/story?id=40866712; accessed on 13 September 2016; *ABC News* is a US news media outlet.

[367] ■ Web site; crocusgroup.com; "News and Announcements"; www.crocusgroup.com/press-center/news/749; Web site is the official page for Crocus Group, one of the leading development companies in Russia.

[368] ■ Online newspaper article; *The Daily Beast*; "Meet The Man Who Is Spinning For Donald Trump In Russia"; 8 September 2016; https://www.thdailybeast.com/articles/2016/09/08/meet-the-man-who-spinning-for-donald-trump-in-russia.html; accessed on 13 September 2016; *The Daily Beast* is an online news outlet.

[369] ■ Online newspaper article; *The Daily Beast*; "Meet The Man Who Is Spinning For Donald Trump In Russia"; 8 September 2016; https://www.thdailybeast.com/articles/2016/09/08/meet-the-man-who-spinning-for-donald-trump-in-russia.html; accessed on 13 September 2016; *The Daily Beast* is an online news outlet.

[370] ■ Online newspaper article; *Sputnik News*; "US Firms 'Unlikely' to Invest in Russia Energy Sector Despite Thaw in Ties"; https://sputniknews.com/business/20160419/1038277709/energy-investments-ties.html; accessed on 12 September 2016; Sputnik News is a Russian state-owned news media outlet.

[371]

[372]

[373]

[374]

[375]

[376]

[377] ■ Online article; *Brightest Young Things*; "What Dreams May Come: A Conversation with Sergei Millian" 31 March 2017; https://www.brightestyoungthings.com/articles/sergei-millian-interview-what-dreams-may-come; Brightest Young Things is an online magazine and event production and marketing agency based in Washington, D.C. and New York City.

[378]

[379]

[380]

[381]

[382] Website; Citizen.org; "Trans-Pacific Partnership (TPP): Expanded Corporate Power, Lower Wages, Unsafe Food Imports"; www.citizen.org/TPP; accessed on 30 November 2016; Citizen.org is the official web site for Public Citizen, a nonprofit policy and lobbying group.

[383]

Report Provided to Journalists, Not FBI
Report Not Provided to Corn

**Date Report Provided to FBI by Steele

384 ████████

385 Website; mcclatchydc.com; "Russian Tech Expert named in Trump report says US intelligence never contacted him"; 11 January 2017; www.mcclatchydc.com/news/nation-world/national/article125910774.html; accessed on 12 January 2017; McClatchy DC is an online media source.

386 Website; XBT; "Company Overview"; www.XBT.com/company-overview.html; accessed on 12 January 2017. XBT is a cyber-resource-based company.

387 Website; XBT; "Geography"; www.XBT.com/geography.html; accessed on 12 January 2017. XBT is a cyber-resource-based company.

388 Website; mcclatchydc.com; "Russian Tech Expert named in Trump report says US intelligence never contacted him"; 11 January 2017; www.mcclatchydc.com/news/nation-world/national/article125910774.html; accessed on 12 January 2017; McClatchy DC is an online media source.

389 Website; XBT; "Company Overview"; www.XBT.com/company-overview.html; accessed on 12 January 2017. XBT is a cyber-resource-based company.

390 Website; XBT; "Geography"; www.XBT.com/geography.html; accessed on 12 January 2017. XBT is a cyber-resource-based company.

*Report Date
**Date Report Provided to FBI by ██Steele██

Report Provided to Journalists, Not FBI
Report Not Provided to Corn

PRODUCED TO SSCI/SSCI

www.ingramcontent.com/pod-product-compliance
Lightning Source LLC
Chambersburg PA
CBHW041653260326

41914CB00018B/1626